MINDSET POWER

A Kid's Guide to Growing Better Every Day

Shannon Anderson

illustrated by Violet Lemay

*To Celia—
Way to
Grow!*

Shannon Anderson

free spirit
PUBLISHING®

Library of Congress Cataloging-in-Publication Data
Names: Anderson, Shannon, 1972– author.
Title: Mindset power : a kid's guide to growing better every day / by Shannon Anderson.
Description: Minneapolis, MN : Free Spirit Publishing, [2020] | Includes bibliographical references and index. | Audience: Ages 9–13.
Identifiers: LCCN 2020005085 (print) | LCCN 2020005086 (ebook) | ISBN 9781631984976 (paperback) | ISBN 9781631984983 (pdf) | ISBN 9781631984990 (epub)
Subjects: LCSH: Attitude (Psychology)—Juvenile literature. | Achievement motivation in children—Juvenile literature.
Classification: LCC BF327 .A534 2020 (print) | LCC BF327 (ebook) | DDC 152.4083—dc23
LC record available at https://lccn.loc.gov/2020005085
LC ebook record available at https://lccn.loc.gov/2020005086

Free Spirit Publishing does not have control over or assume responsibility for author or third-party websites and their content. At the time of this book's publication, all facts and figures cited within are the most current available. All telephone numbers, addresses, and website URLs are accurate and active; all publications, organizations, websites, and other resources exist as described in this book; and all have been verified as of January 2022. If you find an error or believe that a resource listed here is not as described, please contact Free Spirit Publishing. Parents, teachers, and other adults: We strongly urge you to monitor children's use of the internet.

Published in association with Cyle Young of C.Y.L.E. (Cyle Young Literary Elite, LLC), a literary agency.

Reading Level Grade 4; Interest Level Ages 9–13;
Fountas & Pinnell Guided Reading Level R

Edited by Eric Braun
Cover and interior design by Emily Dyer
Illustrated by Violet Lemay

10 9 8 7 6 5 4 3 2
Printed in the United States of America
V20300222

Free Spirit Publishing Inc.
6325 Sandburg Road, Suite 100
Minneapolis, MN 55427-3674
(612) 338-2068
help4kids@freespirit.com
freespirit.com

FSC
www.fsc.org
MIX
Paper from
responsible sources
FSC® C005010

Acknowledgments

I'd like to acknowledge and thank the Free Spirit team for the encouragement, dedication, and work they have given me and this book project. The entire team is instrumental in helping with all of the moving parts, but I want to specifically thank Eric Braun, an amazing editor with a great vision for what will make the pages come alive and the concepts clearer. Judy Galbraith is an incredibly kind and wonderful leader. Margie Lisovskis has answered so many questions and keeps everything organized. Amanda Shofner is super-knowledgeable and supportive in helping to promote the publications we create. This team embraces a growth mindset with every step of the process, and I'm thankful to be a part of their great work!

CONTENTS

INTRODUCTION

Growing Better All the Time

Let's start with a positive thought: You will *never* reach your full potential. Munch on that for a moment . . .

What? You don't think that seems very positive?

This isn't a trick. It actually *is* good news. It's fantastic news! It means you can always keep learning and you don't have to worry about your brain getting too full. The sky is the limit!

You began learning before you were even born. You learned to recognize voices and started developing your senses. You weren't just getting bigger fingers and toes, you were growing your brain. And your brain keeps on growing your whole life—as long as you continue to do things that make it stronger.

One way you and your brain get stronger is by facing challenges. As you go through life, you face a lot of challenges, from little ones to big ones to *super* big ones. Sometimes you might really struggle. Maybe you'll have a hard time with a certain subject in school. When you have a lot of assignments and tests, you may feel overwhelmed trying to keep up. If you play a sport, you'll probably deal with disappointing performances or losses. As you meet new people, you may struggle to figure out how to act or who to hang out with. Maybe you wish you were better at playing the guitar, but learning it is really frustrating. Maybe you love baking, but all your cakes come out flat.

This book will show you how to change the way you think about your challenges so you can grow from them, feel better about yourself, and get better at the things you try.

You can learn to think of your challenges as *opportunities!*

This doesn't mean that you will win every game, get all A's, and be the most popular kid in school. No book can make you perfect, because there are no perfect people. What this book *can* do is help you always improve and believe in yourself.

About This Book

Mindset Power is a guide to help you think about your daily choices in different ways so you can be the best you. By developing positive habits and learning how to use mistakes and failures as a way to grow better, you can do just about anything you set your mind to. That's called having a **growth mindset**, and that's what this book is all about.

Here's what you'll find in *Mindset Power*:

Chapter 1, Change Your Thinking to Change Your Life. Everyone faces struggles and challenges that can cause them to doubt themselves or feel like they aren't capable of certain skills. This chapter shows you that you have the power to choose how you react to challenges. Positive reactions can lead to positive outcomes.

Chapter 2, What Is a Growth Mindset? You'll learn how the right mindset, or mental attitude, can help you overcome setbacks, achieve goals you care about, and believe in yourself.

Chapter 3, Brain Boosting. This chapter is about the brain research behind growth mindset, and also about how to take good care of your brain. Many complex things happen in our minds as we make decisions throughout the day. Learn what to do to help your brain change and grow.

Chapter 4, The Power of Positivity. People feel better and do better when they have—and spread—a positive vibe rather than a negative one. This chapter is packed with ideas for staying positive.

Chapter 5, Setting Your Goals. Setting goals is an important first step in the process of learning something new. This chapter shows you how to set goals and build a plan for success. Without a goal, you don't have a target. Without a target, it's a lot harder to improve and make progress.

Chapter 6, Hocus Pocus, Time to Focus. Once you've set your goals, the next challenge is to stay focused on them. It's easy to get distracted or forget your purpose for working so hard. Read about ways to help you stay on track—and get *back* on track when you lose your way.

Chapter 7, Destination: Determination. There is power in determination. This chapter will give you strategies for sticking with things that are important, even when you have setbacks or make mistakes.

Chapter 8, Your Best Is Yet to Come! This chapter sums up how boosting your brain power, using a growth mindset, staying positive, and focusing on your goals can help you be your best yet.

Be sure to check out the resources in the back of the book. You'll find a list of recommended books and videos with even more information about the power of a growth mindset.

As you read, you'll find lots of opportunities to practice your new skills and write about what you learn. When you see a box that says **JOT YOUR THOUGHTS,** grab a notebook or a device and write your answers to the questions. You'll also find activity forms you can photocopy or print. (All the forms can be downloaded at freespirit.com/mindset.) Boxes titled **SOMETHING TO TRY** provide ideas for practicing what you're learning. All that practice and note-taking will help you process and remember what you learn. And it will help you make progress toward your goals and learn to boost your mindset power.

You'll still face lots of challenges every day. Everyone does! Some of them will feel really big and overwhelming. Challenges, setbacks, disappointments . . . these are all normal parts of life.

They're also how you grow. And with your new skills and a growth mindset, you'll be better able to do just that.

I would love to hear how the ideas in this book work for you. Write to me at the address below. Tell me about how your growth mindset helped you and let me know if you have other strategies.

Shannon Anderson
help4kids@freespirit.com

CHAPTER 1

CHANGE YOUR THINKING TO CHANGE YOUR LIFE

Have you ever had any thoughts like these?

- "It's hard for me to make friends. That's just how I am."

- "I stink at soccer."

- "I'm just not a good reader."

- "I'll never learn how to do long division!"

- "I might as well quit the violin—I'll never be good enough."

Maybe you want to be a great soccer player, but you struggle to get better. Or you love stories and wish you could be a writer, but the idea of becoming a published author seems out of reach. Maybe you want to answer questions in class but are too nervous to raise your hand.

Frustrating Fears and Dastardly Doubts

There are so many hard things you have to work through—at school, at home, in life. Things that can be frustrating and seem unfair. How do you learn to handle this tough stuff?

Jagger wanted to run for student council. Last year, he saw the student council members show new students around, introduce speakers at school assemblies, and organize fundraisers that helped people in his community. Not to mention, they had cool shirts.

Only one student from each classroom got to be a representative. Jagger really wanted to represent his class and be a part of this important club. However, doubt crept in when he realized there were a lot of other kids in his class who would run—kids who were more popular. He thought about how much time it would take to prepare a speech and a poster. He worried that whatever he said in front of his classmates wouldn't be good enough to convince them to pick him over the other kids.

Doubt was almost like a person who was saying things like this to Jagger: "Who do you think you are that *you* should win the election? Don't you know that Abby is running? All of the girls will vote for her. And Lakin, the soccer king, is running too. The jocks will vote for him over you any day. Josh, the brainiest kid in class, is running. He's way smarter than you. Besides, what would you even say in your speech? What if you forget what you're supposed to say? You can't draw. How are you going to make a poster? What if kids laugh at you and your poster? What if they whisper about you while you are talking? You should sit this one out."

Jagger was starting to think the doubt was right. Maybe he shouldn't run for student council.

Jagger was letting his doubts talk him out of trying something he wanted to do. He didn't know if he would win the election, but one thing is for sure: He definitely wouldn't win if he didn't try!

Have you ever experienced something like this? Has doubt or fear "talked" to you and tried to control your thoughts? It can be hard to ignore doubt and fear. They are powerful feelings. Thankfully, you are the boss of your brain. You get to choose what you focus on. Your choices can help or hurt you. For example:

- You have the power to choose how you react when you start to feel doubt or fear.

- You have the power to choose your goals.

- You have the power to choose how hard you work toward those goals.

- You have the power to choose your attitude toward things you have to do, like homework or chores.

In all these cases, your choices can influence how you feel about yourself. Some choices can lead you to feel unhappy or anxious. They can lead you to limit yourself. Other choices can help you feel confident and happier with your outcomes. Those choices can help you face your problems with strategies that point you toward solutions.

Talking Back to Negative Feelings

When Jagger's doubts were "talking" to him, he felt uncertain. What if he could talk back to his doubt and tell it to go away?

Jagger realized he was letting negative feelings hold him back from trying something he really wanted to do. So he decided to talk back to his doubt—literally. He typed the following letter:

```
Dear Doubt,

You don't know that all of the girls
will vote for Abby just because
she's a girl. Boys won't vote for
Lakin just because he is good at
soccer. Even though Josh is really
smart, he doesn't have a better
chance than I do if I work hard.

No one will even see who votes for
which candidates, so kids will
probably vote for the person they
think will do the best job, not who
is the most popular or the smartest.
```

I want to be a candidate for important reasons, and it means enough to me to practice hard and get some help on my poster. If I mess up my speech, I can clear my throat and keep going. If I mess up my poster, I can start over on the back side. People will see my desire to do well and the hard work I put in, and that is what gives me a good chance at winning. If I don't run for the position, I have no chance at all.

So, Mr. Doubt, you can just go away. I won't be needing you. I've got some work to do.

(Not) Your friend,
Jagger

Jagger still didn't know how he would do in the election, but he chose to give it a shot. Win or lose, he would know that he tried hard, and that made him feel good about himself.

When you learn more about the power of your own choices, you can start to feel better about yourself too. Whether you want to make your own graphic novel or beat your dad at chess, you have the power to choose your attitude. That's what a growth mindset is all about.

JOT YOUR THOUGHTS

Think of a time you had a doubt or fear that took over your thoughts and caused you to question yourself. Write a letter to that doubt or fear, telling it why you don't believe what it's saying to you. Write about all the positive reasons you should take a chance anyway.

CHAPTER 2

WHAT IS A GROWTH MINDSET?

You know what growth is. You've seen plants, your pets, your siblings, and even your friends grow. Take a moment to think about what a *mindset* is.

A mindset is a particular way of thinking about something. It can be your attitude or sets of opinions. People can have either a **fixed** mindset or a **growth** mindset. What do you think the difference is?

Having a fixed mindset means you have decided, once and for all, that you can or can't do something. You believe you can't change your abilities or intelligence. You're convinced that you are pretty much stuck being at the same level, or that you are a certain kind of person. These are some examples of fixed-mindset thinking:

"I can't draw."

"I'm bad at making friends."

"I'm not an athlete."

"I'm not good at geography."

Now that you know what a fixed mindset is, you can probably guess what a growth mindset is. A growth mindset is believing that you have the ability to grow your intelligence and that you *can* become more artistic, athletic, creative, and smart. Even if you don't believe you're very good at it now, you believe you can get better. The best part is that having a growth mindset can unleash the power for you to get better! Here are some examples of growth-mindset thinking:

> *My drawings don't look great yet, but I know I can improve. If I watch drawing videos and practice hard, my brain will start to make more connections.*

> *I'm learning more states and capitals every day. With practice, I will get better at geography.*

> *Even though I haven't made as many friends as I'd like, I am a good person and good friend. I can practice social skills so other kids will start to see that.*

> *Sports don't come naturally to me, but I can exercise and keep practicing. I will work on improving my own performance instead of comparing myself to others.*

You are not only a growth-mindset person or only a fixed-mindset person. You simply choose different mindsets about things you try to do. You might think you are bad at card games, so you have a fixed mindset about that. But at the same time, you might believe in your ability to get better at video games. There could be lots of reasons for these different mindsets. Maybe you have seen yourself improve at video games, so it's easier for you to have a growth mindset about them. But if you have never beaten your sister at gin rummy, it might be hard for you to see how you've gotten better at it.

If you have a fixed mindset, you can work on changing it. When you do, you will have more opportunities to improve at skills and try new things. That's because a fixed mindset can lead you to give up, but a growth mindset can lead you to *open* up—to new experiences, new opportunities, and new successes!

Jessie had always been interested in music. She loved listening to it and talking about it with her friends, and she dreamed that one day she'd be able to play her own songs on the guitar. When her uncle let her borrow his guitar, Jessie got excited. When her stepmom signed her up for lessons, Jessie was thrilled! She was on her way to being a musician.

After her first couple of lessons, though, her fingers started to hurt from pressing the strings. She was supposed to practice for 30 minutes a day, but the music she made didn't sound very good. The chords were difficult to learn. She practiced less and less, and finally she just stopped. Jessie told her stepmom, "I'm just not good at playing music."

Ayden loved their dad's cakes and cookies and often helped him in the kitchen. Ayden decided it would be fun to make cupcakes and cookies for the upcoming bake sale for the scout troop. But when the oven timer went off, the cookies were burnt around the edges. Dad asked if Ayden wanted him to take over.

"No thanks!" Ayden said. "I figured out what I did wrong, and I will be sure to preheat the oven and watch the clock better next time. Besides, I can eat the middles of my mistakes while I make a new batch!"

Jessie had wanted to play the guitar for a long time, but she gave it up pretty easily when it got hard. If she doesn't try again, she'll never know if playing music could add pleasure to her life. Ayden also had a setback, but was able to roll with it. Having a growth mindset gave Ayden a second chance.

Gradual Growth

A growth mindset gives you a positive attitude about growing your skills and abilities. By believing in yourself, you propel yourself toward finding ways to improve. You seek out opportunities to learn. You also realize that getting better at something takes time and consistent practice.

Think about your teeth. You couldn't neglect your teeth for months and then just brush your teeth the day of a dentist appointment and hope for a good checkup. You have to brush them twice a day every day to fight off cavities all year long. It's a practice that needs to be repeated to keep your teeth healthy and strong.

The same is true for just about anything you want to do well. Deciding to improve isn't all there is to it. You can't wake up one morning, decide, *I will learn Spanish today*, and suddenly speak it perfectly. (That would be awesome, wouldn't it?) But that's not how learning works. Instead, remember the *growth* part of growth mindset. It means you can gradually grow your brain to improve. It *is* very possible to learn a number of words in Spanish in one day. And some more the next day. And some more the day after that. You can get a little better every day.

Part of having a growth mindset about something is looking for ways to gradually build that something up. If you decide to take on a big task like learning a new language, you might start by asking yourself questions like these:

- What kind of class or foreign language club could I sign up for?
- What kind of app could I use to practice daily?
- Who speaks the language well and could help me practice?
- Who do I know who also wants to learn the language so we can practice together?
- What movie or show could I watch in that language?

The answers to those questions can give you the information you need to make a plan to tackle your goal. You'll learn more about breaking down goals into smaller steps in chapter 5.

A QUIZ-icle Look at Growth Mindset

As experts do more research about growth mindset, we're all learning more exciting news about our ability to develop our skills and talents. Some of this research wasn't around when your teachers and parents or other family adults were your age. You might even catch them saying things that seem more like a fixed mindset. You may want to share some of what you learn in this book with them!

Page 19 has a short quiz you can take to see what you already know (or don't know) about growth mindset, and to help you understand it better. Don't worry, you won't be graded! Go to freespirit.com/mindset to print the quiz, or just write the numbers 1–10 in your notebook or device and write your answers there. After you finish, check out the answers on pages 20–27 to learn more.

Growth Mindset Quiz (Just for Fun!)

For each question, circle Agree or Disagree.

1. Saying "I'm awesome at piano" is growth-mindset thinking. — Agree   **Disagree**

2. Your brain has the ability to change and get smarter. — Agree   **Disagree**

3. "You're so smart!" is a great thing to say to someone to help them develop a growth mindset. — Agree   **Disagree**

4. If you have a learning disability or are in the gifted program at your school, you should embrace these labels as who you are. — Agree   **Disagree**

5. You can lose some of your knowledge and skills. — Agree   **Disagree**

6. Many famous, successful people claim their success is due to their failures. — Agree   **Disagree**

7. The best kind of practice is when you practice specific skills that need improvement. — Agree   **Disagree**

8. People who are extremely talented are just very lucky. — Agree   **Disagree**

9. Your grades are a good way to predict your potential to learn. — Agree   **Disagree**

10. You inherit your weaknesses from your parents. — Agree   **Disagree**

Now that you've finished the quiz, let's take a look at the mindsets behind each of the statements in it.

1. **Saying "I'm awesome at piano" is growth-mindset thinking.**

This one was a bit of a trick. Even though it's a positive statement, saying you are awesome at something is actually a fixed-mindset way of thinking. That's because by saying that you are already great at it, you suggest that you can't or won't get better. You may, in fact, be very good at playing the piano, but to apply a growth mindset, you'd need to change how you look at your success.

You could say, "I'm definitely on the right track with my piano playing" or "I'm improving so much as I practice." Or "Now that I'm doing so well, I'm excited to play some different musical styles, like jazz." This shift in thinking encourages you to keep learning and improving.

2. **Your brain has the ability to change and get smarter.**
You'll learn more about this idea in chapter 3, Brain Boosting.
For now, the main thing to know is that your brain *does* have the
ability to grow and change physically. And these changes in your
brain are connected to your ability to grow your intelligence. It
has to do with strengthening connections between special nerve
cells called *neurons*. Developing stronger connections causes your
neurons to work together more quickly and automatically.

3. **"You're so smart!" is a great thing to say to someone to
help that person develop a growth mindset.**
Maybe someone has said this to you. Or you may have said it to
someone else. It does *seem* like a compliment—and most people
mean it that way. However, telling people they are smart really isn't
giving them credit for the time, effort, and practice that went into
their learning. A more powerful compliment to help someone grow
would be, "Wow! You worked really hard on that and never gave up!"

Praising Effort Leads to Growth

Researchers say the most helpful praise is focused on effort, not
intelligence. If we tell people we think they are smart, they may not
challenge themselves to do harder things.

Psychologist Carol Dweck did some experiments that showed
this. Kids who were praised for being smart tended to develop more
of a fixed mindset, whereas kids who were praised for working hard
wanted to continue to be challenged. They had a growth mindset
that connected their beliefs about the effort they put in with the
results they achieved. They actually worked harder and made greater
improvements because the feedback they received was tied to their
efforts. This hard work continued to help them make progress.

4. **If you have a learning disability or are in the gifted program at your school, you should embrace the labels as who you are.**

This statement is all about labels that we are sometimes given at school. You may be an English-language learner, someone with dyslexia, someone who has a hearing impairment, someone who is gifted, someone who has ADHD, or someone with any number of descriptions. But these labels or descriptions don't define YOU. They are simply a part of you, and they don't take away your ability to grow your brain or develop skills. It may take you more or less time than others to master a skill, or you may be able to learn things with more or less practice. We all can learn, though, as long as we keep a growth mindset.

5. **You can lose some of your knowledge and skills.**

This is kind of a bummer. We *can* lose skills and forget things that we learn. If you've ever heard the phrase "Use it or lose it," you can believe it. Just as your brain can grow and develop stronger neural connections, those connections can also weaken if you don't practice or continue to learn.

If you play chess for a year in elementary school and then never practice it again until college, chances are you will have forgotten many of the rules and moves you learned. On the bright side, you can work toward making those connections strong again.

6. **Many famous, successful people claim their success is due to their failures.**

Yes, they do, and this is very inspirational. It can seem like really talented people have always had the ability to do what they do. It's true that some people may have a natural talent or physical advantage, but most have to develop skills over time. Everyone who is considered an expert or master was a beginner at some point. They struggled, made mistakes, and failed. But they learned from that and kept working. And that's why they eventually succeeded.

> Think about this quote from famous soccer player Pelé: "Success is no accident. It is hard work, perseverance, learning, studying, sacrifice, and most of all, love of what you are doing or learning to do."
>
> This pretty much sums up what it takes to get really good at anything. Trials are part of the process.

7. The best kind of practice is when you practice specific skills that need improvement.

True. All practice isn't created equally. You have to purposefully plan out *what kind* of practice will get you to your goals. For example, if you want to learn how to do a back walk-over in gymnastics, you have to practice skills that build toward that. If you only practice cartwheels and round-offs, you won't move any closer to your goal, because cartwheels and round-offs don't develop the flexibility or the muscle movements you need to do a back walk-over. Instead, you would have to practice steps that are part of a back walk-over and skills that develop those steps. You would start with back bends and pushing up from the ground. Next, you'd work on going into a back bend from a standing position, then work your way into practicing the kick-over and standing back upright. This applies to anything you want to learn.

Choose to practice in ways that specifically challenge you to improve at that thing.

8. **People who are extremely talented are just very lucky.** This is a phrase you may have heard before: "He's so lucky to be that artistically talented." "She's so lucky that she's a star softball player." But luck is really only a small part of talent. Most people who we see as extremely talented have probably worked a lot behind the scenes to develop that talent.

Even if you inherit traits that make you more or less able to learn something, you still have to put in time and practice. Maybe you were born with physical features, like being tall, that give you an advantage shooting baskets or playing volleyball. Maybe you were born with fast-twitch muscle fibers that help you run fast. Or you could have inherited your mom's good genes for singing. None of those inherited traits can automatically make you great at that thing.

In most cases, a person who seems lucky to have success—whether it's in a sport, hobby, leadership position, or something else—got there through a lot of different factors. The person may have inherited some helpful traits, or may have grown up with a family who supported their goals, dreams, and efforts. The person probably also had a lot of determination and growth mindset, meeting those goals through hard work.

All his life, **Marco** had been surrounded by art and encouraged to do art-related activities. He often went to art museums and took classes. He also learned from his mother, who was a painter herself. Marco loved drawing and painting, so he spent a lot of time doing that. He had dreams of illustrating books when he got older.

Marco's classmates voted for him to draw the class mural in the hallway. When he was finished, everyone loved it. "That's beautiful," said Eliana. "I wish I was good at drawing. You're lucky."

Marco *was* good at art, but it wasn't because he was just lucky. It's true he was fortunate to have the opportunities he had in his life, but his ability to do well came from his experiences with art, studying art, and practicing it.

9. **Your grades are a good way to predict your potential to learn.**
Grades are used to let you, your parents or guardians, and other adults know roughly how you are performing based on the work you've done and your teacher's judgment. But grades don't tell you much about what you are capable of, or your potential.

Please don't let the grade you receive for a subject put you into a fixed mindset for that subject. You can get a grade you don't like in math and still get better grades in the future. You might even become a successful engineer one day. A low grade is not taking into account the growth you have made in that subject so far. You may just need more time, a different learning style, or additional practice. A low grade does not mean you are *bad* at math.

10. You inherit your weaknesses from your parents.

The environment you grow up in can influence what you like to do or your attitude toward doing it, but it doesn't mean you will have the same strengths or weaknesses as your mom or dad.

For example, maybe your dad struggled with math in school, didn't take higher math, and doesn't feel confident in his abilities in math. If that's true, you may grow up thinking math is too hard as well. Maybe you've heard him say things like, "Math is not my thing, have your big sister help you with your homework." If your dad has negative feelings about math, he might not have encouraged you to dive into number puzzles and learn cool multiplication tricks.

None of that means you don't have the ability to do math well. It may just mean you don't have much positive experience with it. You weren't born unable to do well in math just because your dad didn't get good grades in it.

Which Way Do You Lean?

Think about your own thinking habits. Do you usually tend more toward a fixed mindset or a growth mindset? How easy is it to change your mindset?

People who have a growth mindset about learning will start to seek information about the skill they are working on. They search for ways to grow and learn, and they recognize that the way they learn may be different from the way someone else learns in terms of time and effort. Their goals are focused on making specific gains. They concentrate on taking action and training their brain to do hard things.

With fixed-mindset thinking, people believe their abilities are limited, and they may let fear of failure control what they take on. Often, people with a fixed mindset are more worried about *looking* smart than actually *getting* smart, so they don't take risks. They view mistakes as disasters rather than chances to learn and readjust. Instead of thinking about how much they could learn from a challenge, they first decide if they will succeed or fail. If there is any risk of failure, they won't try it.

Fill out the short survey on the next page to help you see your own leanings toward a growth mindset or a fixed mindset. Being aware of your tendencies can help you make better mindset choices in the future. Go to freespirit.com/mindset to print a copy of the survey, or just write your answers in your notebook or device.

Survey: Fixed or Growth Mindset

You might have a fixed mindset in some areas and a growth mindset in others. Or, like many people, you may have habits and tendencies that make you lean one way or the other overall. These questions can help you start thinking about how you think. Put a check mark under the most appropriate answer for each question.

	Almost Always	Usually	Not Often	Never
1. Do you give up when something frustrates you to the point of grouchiness?				
2. Do you avoid asking questions in class for fear people will think you are not smart or weren't paying attention?				
3. Do you believe your brain stays the same once you stop growing?				
4. Do you avoid trying new strategies if you don't understand them?				
5. Do you believe that smart people don't have to try as hard?				
6. Do you believe failures are permanent?				
7. Do you often hide your mistakes?				

$\longrightarrow$

Survey: Fixed or Growth Mindset continued

If most of your answers are "Almost Always" or "Usually," you may have more of a fixed mindset. If most of your answers are "Not Often" or "Never," you may have more of a growth mindset. What if you answered with some of each? You may have a mixed mindset—your mindset can go either way depending on the situation.

If you find that you have more of a fixed mindset, or a mixed one, this book will help you to gravitate over to the growth side. The more you know, the more you grow. The more you grow, the smarter you are! If you find that you lean toward a growth mindset, this book can give you even more tools to accomplish your goals with a positive attitude. You are on the right track to being the best you!

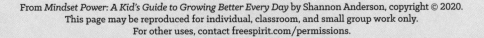

Turning Setbacks into Set-UPs

The last two questions in the survey on page 28 are about failures and mistakes. How you think about setbacks is a really important part of your mindset. Are you encouraged when you make a mistake and learn from it, or do you look at a mistake as a failure?

Holden and **Joshua** were working on a crossword puzzle at their grandmother's apartment. They were both really stuck on number six down. After trying several words, Holden threw his hands up. "We'll never get this thing figured out!"

"Wait a minute!" Joshua said. "I see what happened. We have two across wrong. That's messing up the letter clues for six down."

"Oh, great," Holden said. "*Two* mistakes. Like I said, we're never going to finish. We're not good at this puzzle stuff."

"But this mistake is a good thing," Joshua said. "When we fix two across, we'll have new clues for all these other words, including six down." After a minute, Joshua tried a new word for two across. It worked. He and Holden looked at the clue for six down and compared it to its spot in the puzzle. With some brainstorming, they figured out the answer.

"All right!" Holden said, smiling.

"We're making progress now," said Joshua. "I'm glad we found that important mistake."

Joshua discovered he and Holden had the wrong word going across and got excited because finding this mistake would help with the rest of the puzzle. But Holden got frustrated about the wrong word—he chose to think the mistake meant they weren't smart enough to do the puzzle. He saw it as a signal to stop, rather than an opportunity to learn how to improve.

You can choose how you think about setbacks. Seeing them as progress is growth-mindset thinking. Not only does that help you learn from the setback and find a solution to what you're doing, but it can be a lot more fun too!

Setbacks can set you UP for success.

If you learn only one thing from this whole book, make it this: How well you do while you're in the process of learning a new skill does not make you a good or a bad person. It doesn't make you a smart or a dumb person. It simply does not define you.

If you don't figure something out on the first few tries, that doesn't mean you will never get it. Your ability to learn is limitless. You will only find out how much time and effort it will take to learn something if you try.

Solcy enjoyed playing with her puppy, Harry, and wanted a new way to bond with him. She decided to teach him how to jump through a Hula-Hoop, like dogs she saw on YouTube. She got out her hoop and had her brother, **Naza**, hold it up. Then she snapped her fingers at Harry and pointed at the hoop, showing him to jump through. But each time Harry got close to the hoop, he turned and ran away.

Solcy was disappointed. "Harry's too scared of the hoop and not smart enough," she said.

Naza agreed. "Too bad," he said. "I guess he'll never learn any tricks."

But the more Solcy thought about it, the more she wanted to make this work. "Today was frustrating," she said to Naza. "But I bet we can find a way to teach him. We just need more information."

Solcy and Naza went to the library and checked out a book about teaching dogs tricks involving props. Reading the book, Solcy realized a mistake she had made. She needed to allow Harry to get used to the hoop before ever trying to do anything with it. She laid it on the ground in the living room for the rest of the evening so Harry could go over to it on his own. She praised him and gave him bites of kibble whenever he touched it with his nose or paw.

In the morning, Solcy held the hoop up for Harry to jump through. Harry wasn't scared this time, but he didn't understand what he was supposed to do. Solcy went back to reading the book and learned that she needed to teach Harry about walking through the hoop while it was touching the ground.

Sure enough, when Naza held the hoop upright, resting on the ground, and Solcy held a treat on the other side, Harry walked through to get the treat. They practiced this many times that day. The next day, they started again at the beginning. They laid the hoop on the ground, let Harry sniff it, and had him walk through several times. Then Naza raised it up about an inch off the ground. Harry could still walk through at this height with no problems.

Harry was enjoying this opportunity to earn treats and make his favorite people so happy. When Naza started raising the hoop up a couple inches, gradually increasing the height over time, Harry learned to jump through to get his treat on the other side. When he did, Solcy hugged him and told him he was a good doggy. Harry wagged his tail and licked her face.

Solcy started to slip into a fixed mindset when teaching Harry a trick didn't work at first. She almost gave up before she even learned what her mistakes were. But instead she made an important decision: she decided to change to a growth mindset. Teaching Harry a trick was important to her, so she learned more about how to do it. With more information, she was able to figure out her mistakes, try different strategies, and eventually succeed. Her hard work and persistence paid off. Now Solcy and Harry have a trick they can enjoy for many years.

Even when you feel really down about the thing you're doing, and you have a big, fat fixed mindset, you have it in you to choose a different way of thinking. You can change to a growth mindset. That's a powerful choice! It really can change your life when you don't give up and keep trying.

Take a look at the form on the next page, "In a Fix . . . or Growing Strong?" It asks you to think about some of the times you have a fixed mindset or growth mindset. You can answer these in your notebook or device, or go to freespirit.com/mindset and print out the form. Either way, keep your answers so you can look at them later. Are there some areas you would like to change your thinking? Do you think you can do it?

(Hint: Yes you can!)

In a Fix . . . or Growing Strong?

In a Fix

What are some things that you have a fixed mindset about? Consider sports, projects, or instruments you've tried and found difficult. Think about skills you don't think you have or will ever have. Are there any things you find challenging but would like to try? Write down as many ideas as you can think of.

Now look at your list. Pick one or two that you would like to learn to do well. In what ways have you tried to work on them? What happened that made you feel like you weren't able to improve?

Growing Strong

What are some things that you have a growth mindset about? List a few skills or hobbies that you feel confident about your ability to get better at.

$\longrightarrow$

In a Fix … or Growing Strong? continued

Choose one item from your list. Why do you think you have a growth mindset about it?

How do you continue to challenge yourself to improve in that skill or hobby? What more can you do to keep getting better?

How can you apply the positive lessons from your "Growing Strong" activity (growth mindset) to the item or items on your "In a Fix" (fixed mindset) list?

CHAPTER 3

BRAIN BOOSTING

Your brain is the only organ in your body that has the ability to make decisions. It's super powerful. It can complete many complicated, amazing tasks at once, and do them well. From what to study or eat to what to say, your brain controls all the choices you make. It even takes care of many things automatically, like your breathing. For most people, it is mysterious and difficult to understand how the brain can control so much.

Your brain is much more powerful than the biggest, most modern computer ever made. But, much like a computer programmer who wants to learn how a computer works so they can get it to function at a high level, you can learn how your brain works in order to get it to perform at a high level. You can get better at the things you want to get better at by understanding the science behind your brain.

An Inside Look at Your Brain

You have billions of nerve cells called *neurons* throughout your body. The neurons in your brain receive input from neurons elsewhere in your body and make decisions about what to do. Then the brain's neurons send messages back out to the rest of the neurons, telling the body how to respond. Those neurons in your brain control everything you think, do, and feel. They are very busy!

Neurons send messages to one another through the synapses, or pathways, between them. As you learn, you may repeat an action or thought many times. This causes the same brain neurons to "fire," or send signals, through the same synapses again and again. When this happens, the synapses carry the signals faster. There is a saying about these neural pathways: "What fires together, wires together." This means that when you do something many times, you don't have to think about it as much. It becomes more automatic. The neurons "learn" what to do.

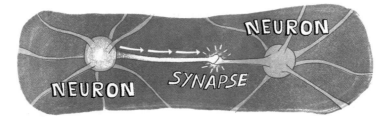

Have you ever read about a character or setting in a story that reminded you of something from your own life? Or have you heard someone talk about visiting a place and been reminded of a time you visited the very same place? By revisiting and thinking about these memories in your brain and connecting them to new experiences and memories, you strengthen the synapses that connect your neurons to each other. These connections can then carry more messages throughout your brain when you need them.

Your thoughts and memories can strengthen your synapses between neurons. If you see a picture of your grandmother, it can cause sensory neurons associated with those memories to activate. For example, you may think about the sound of her voice or the smell of her famous home-baked cookies. Thinking about her causes your sensory neurons to react in the same ways they did when she was around, making those synapses stronger. That keeps your memories of her stronger. If you stop thinking about her over time, those synapses will weaken and you will forget her more and more. It will be harder to trigger those pathways once they are weak.

Another way you can think of creating neural pathways is trudging through snow to walk down the sidewalk after a storm. Maybe you are the first person to venture out. It could be really tough to get through all of the high drifts and loose, powdery spots. There may be no path there at all. If you return to that same path, though, you can pack down the snow each time you use the route. Over time, your footing will get better as you make a more solid, defined path.

When you are learning new skills or information, it can feel like you are blazing a new trail through the snow. You may think every step is slippery and tricky. As you trudge through, you can pack down a path that works for you so that, each time you walk the path, it starts to be clearer where to navigate and easier to walk without falling.

> The term for the brain's ability to grow and change is **neuroplasticity**. The first part, *neuro*, means "related to the brain." *Plasticity* refers to the ability to change. Neuroplasticity happens when you learn new things through practice, intentional repetition, and effort.

Use It or Lose It!

You now know that practicing skills makes the synapses in your brain stronger. The opposite is also true. If you stop using skills for a while, you can actually weaken those pathways and lose some of the most basic skills you once had.

If you stop practicing something, your brain recognizes that those synapses are not being used regularly, and it will stop using them. In this way, the brain can become more efficient and powerful by putting energy into strengthening the synapses you do use—and shedding unnecessary connections. It's a form of "survival of the fittest" in your brain.

When you learn something in class, your neurons send signals through certain synapses. If you practice what you learned again that evening, the same neurons fire again, causing them to reconnect on the same synapses, making them stronger. If you continue to practice and repeat this the next day, you will continue to make the learning more permanent. However, if you don't think again about the information you learned in the next day or two, you may forget it.

Last summer, **Mae** stayed with her cousin **Lee** for a couple weeks. While she was there, Lee taught her how to play a board game called mancala. The two cousins played the game each evening after supper for the whole two weeks. By the end of her visit, Mae had figured out several strategies for the game, and she even beat Lee a few times. She was proud of her ability to figure out clever new moves. "You have outsmarted me at my own game!" Lee said.

Mae didn't see her cousin again during the school year—and she didn't play mancala either. When she arrived for her visit the next summer, she was excited. "Let's play mancala!" she said. But when she and Lee sat down at the board, Mae was surprised to realize she had forgotten most of the rules and strategies she had learned so well last year. Lee had to reteach her, and it took several games before Mae was able to score. But by the end of the visit, their games were tight and competitive again.

This time when they left, Mae asked her mom for her own mancala set. "I want to keep playing so I keep getting better. Next year I'll give Lee a real challenge!"

If Mae had kept playing mancala regularly, her neural connections would have been stronger. This would have allowed her to play well during the second visit without having to relearn what she knew before. She was able to develop some of those connections faster than if she had *never* played before, but it still took some time and practice to build them up to the strength they once were.

Another example of this happens every summer. Students who have two or three months off for summer break often lose some of their reading and math skills because they don't use them much. If kids don't practice reading and math skills over the summer months, their connections get weaker. When school starts back up again, they have to review and sometimes relearn many of the skills from the year before.

Many schools have gone to a year-round schedule for exactly this reason. These schools still complete the same number of school days, but the days are spread out with more breaks throughout the year and a shorter summer break. Research shows that this helps kids remember more of the information they learn. And it avoids having to waste time relearning when school is back in session.

Neurons increase, weaken, or change on a daily basis. The brain you woke up with this morning is different from the brain you have right now. With each decision you make and experience you have, you can strengthen the signals your neurons send and receive. As these strengthen, they make you "smarter."

Building Skills on Top of Skills

When you are young, you learn lots of important skills. For example, you learn how to read. You learn basic math facts. Once

SOMETHING TO TRY

1. Draw a big bumpy oval on a sheet of paper. This represents your brain.

2. Inside the brain you sketched, draw nine or ten neuron cells. They can just look like big dots or circles, or you can have fun making them more interesting. Spread them out throughout the brain so there is space between them.

3. Think of something you have practiced a lot and consider yourself pretty good at. Draw a thick line connecting two of the neurons. Label that line with the skill you are good at.

4. Now think of something you are still learning but aren't as good at yet. Draw a thinner line between two other neurons. Label that line with the skill you are still learning.

5. Finally, think of something you have just started learning. Maybe you have just been introduced to that skill. Draw a dotted line connecting two neurons and label it with this new skill.

This exercise can help you visualize what is going on in your brain with your neurons, depending on how well you can do or learn something. If you stopped practicing the skill you labeled for your thick line, that line could eventually get thinner or even disappear. On the other hand, if you keep practicing and challenging yourself with those new skills, you can make the line much thicker.

you've been in school for several years, though, the challenges become different. You start applying the skills you've learned to accomplish harder things. Instead of learning to read, you are reading to learn. Instead of memorizing your math facts, you *use* those facts to solve math problems. And instead of figuring out how to spell words, you use words to express yourself in writing. When you apply a skill you've already learned to new learning, it strengthens your use and mastery of the first skill as well as the new one. More repetition, more mastery!

Can you think of things you learned in your younger years that you use today to do something more complicated? For example, you probably learned the alphabet song to learn the names of the letters in order. Then you learned what those letters look like, and you started to learn what sound each letter makes. From there, you strung together groups of letters to form words. These words were used to form sentences, and so on.

The basics of learning something new, like your letters and sounds, are called *foundational skills.* Maybe you've heard of the foundation of a building. When a new building is constructed, the builders dig a big hole in the ground and put the strongest part of the building there. That's the foundation, and it has to be strong enough to hold up the whole building. Without a solid foundation, the building will eventually become uneven and sink in places where the ground settles. Worse, the roof and walls could start cracking, unable to support the weight without the solid concrete foundation to rest on.

Knowing the alphabet lays a foundation for you to learn the patterns necessary to eventually read and write. Each time you build on your foundational skills, you strengthen the neural connections in your brain. Once you have a strong foundation, you don't even really have to think about those skills. When was the last time you wrote a sentence and thought about the sound each letter makes to spell out every word? What about tying your shoes? If you've done it enough times, it seems like your hands just know what to do.

Many things you do now require foundational skills. Maybe you play the trumpet. The first things you probably had to learn were how to hold the instrument and what all of the parts were. Then you learned how to blow into it. You had to learn the names of the notes and then how to make each note's sound. Once you practiced awhile, the holding and the parts and the notes became part of your foundational skills. Building upon and practicing those skills has begun to form strong neural connections in your brain. You can continue to strengthen these pathways as you practice harder notes and songs and push yourself to work on them.

JOT YOUR THOUGHTS

Write down a few skills you know how to do. They might be sports-related skills, cooking skills, musical skills, solving a certain kind of puzzle, fishing, sewing, or anything that requires some learning and practice.

Pick one of those skills and think about what went into learning it. How did you start? What are the foundational skills you started with? How did you build on those foundational skills?

Strategies for Building Strong Brain Connections

So, how can you build stronger neural connections? Here are a few tips and strategies.

Practice

Of course! But practice doesn't just mean doing the same thing over and over. You need to practice meaningfully in ways that challenge your brain to work hard. You build new skills by choosing the specific areas you need to improve. If you know how to make a yo-yo go up and down but want to get better at new tricks, you have to practice the tricks. It won't make you better at "Walk the Dog" or "Around the World" if you *only* practice the simple up-and-down motion. Set aside some time each day to practice the tricks you want to learn until you are able to perform them smoothly.

In order to *keep* getting better, you have to practice gradually harder, more complicated tasks. With the yo-yo, that might mean trying more intricate tricks. If you want to be a stronger reader, it can mean picking up more advanced books. With the saxophone, it can mean playing trickier songs. Maybe you'll even challenge yourself to play a solo in the nextband concert!

SOMETHING TO TRY

Test out your brain's ability to make neural pathways with a ten-day challenge. Choose an activity that will require some practice and work without being overwhelming. Here are some ideas:

- Memorize a poem.

- Learn the sign language alphabet.

- Learn to juggle.

- Memorize the capitals for all the states or provinces and territories.

- Say the alphabet backwards in less than 30 seconds.

- Count to 50 in a foreign language.

- Learn to write the Roman numerals up to 50 from memory.

Practice your activity for ten minutes each day for ten days. Don't skip any days or do less than ten minutes! Each day when you finish practicing, write about how it went. What was hard about it? What did you learn? How far did you get? Can you tell if it was easier than the day before?

Even if you don't master your chosen skill after ten days, chances are you will make major improvements.

Focus on Purpose

When you're practicing a skill or working on an assignment, sometimes it's tempting to just *think about* getting it done. You focus more on finishing the work than you do on *why* you're doing the work. Let's say you want to learn a yo-yo trick, so you decide to practice the trick for ten minutes a day. But if you don't focus on what you're learning—and instead you pay more attention to the clock, thinking more about just *finishing* those ten minutes—you won't learn as well.

More often this happens with things that are not as fun for you as a hobby you're doing for yourself. Maybe your teacher assigned you something to learn in math. If your goal is just to finish the worksheet, thinking this hard thing will go away once you're done, you may regret it later. That's because in school, the skills continue to build upon each other. The skills you're practicing on that worksheet not only won't go away, but they could also get more complex. It's best to learn the basics the first time around instead of running the risk of getting behind.

Think back to when you had to learn your multiplication facts. If you struggled with this skill and did just enough to get by (or if you copied someone else's work), you made things harder for yourself later. You may have felt relieved when the teacher moved on to division, thinking, *Good! That multiplication stuff is over!* But you soon found out that you need multiplication to check your division problems. And eventually you'll have to multiply fractions and decimals too. Multiplication is a foundational skill that you keep using and building on.

This happens in almost all subjects in school and all areas of your life. If you don't understand something, it is best for your grades and your brain to ask questions, practice more, and really learn a skill before moving on. Your teachers want you to let them know when you need more help. They would rather take more time explaining now than move on if you haven't figured it out.

Pay Attention to Feedback

Another tip for growing a strong brain is to pay attention to the feedback you get from family adults, teachers, coaches, and friends. Advice and coaching help you see and understand things you may not notice on your own. Help or another point of view from people with more experience can boost your chances of learning successfully. Listen to their suggestions and try to put them into action.

If you're working on something without a teacher or coach, and you want to get better, seek out feedback. Is there a teacher, parent, neighbor, friend, or family member who knows about that skill? Could you ask them to take a look at your work or creation and give helpful suggestions or their opinions?

You can even ask for help from someone your own age or a little older. If you want to learn how to curve a soccer kick, ask a teammate who knows how to do it to watch you or teach you. If you want to write better, ask a friend who blogs to read some of your work. These kids can give you feedback from the point of view of a person who recently learned and is still building that skill.

Take Care of Your Brain

To grow and boost the brain, you have to take care of it. If you're going to challenge it and feed it more knowledge, you have to give it high-quality fuel and rest.

You can't pour lemonade into the gas tank of a car if you want it to run. In the same way, you can't eat candy bars and potato chips to prepare for thinking and growing. Nutrition is important if you want your brain to be able to perform its best. Lots of foods are beneficial for your brain, like eggs, nuts, fruits, and vegetables. Natural foods with dark, rich colors such as spinach, peppers, squash, berries, and salmon are great for your brain. Think about the colors of the rainbow. The more colorful your plate, the more variety of nutrients you are getting. Choose nuts instead of a sugary snack bar. Choose fruit instead of candy. Eat whole-grain bread instead of white bread if you have the choice. You can research other super brain foods online.

Your brain is mostly made up of water. That means it's important to drink plenty of water every day. Brain cells need lots of water to function properly and for you to stay focused. Even your memory is affected if you don't drink enough.

Your brain needs rest in the form of good sleep. Kids aged 9 to 12 need about 10 hours of sleep every day. Your brain responds best if you go to bed at the same time and wake up at the same time every day—even on weekends.

Last of all, you need some physical exercise to keep a healthy brain. Exercise sends more oxygen and blood to your brain, so it is more alert. This can help with memory and learning new information.

Moving around is also a great way to give your mind a break from all of that thinking and analyzing! Taking a walk outside can take your mind off a difficult task and give you some fresh air at the same time. Sometimes you get your best ideas when you are out on a bike ride, taking a jog, playing on the sidewalk or playground, or doing push-ups. Exercise increases your body's production of feel-good chemicals called endorphins, which help give you positive feelings and can improve your mood. It may be just what you need to help you come up with new ideas for a project.

Endorphins are natural chemicals in the body that fight pain when you are hurt. They are also increased when you exercise and when you laugh! Endorphins are good because they make people feel happy and less stressed.

A Recap on Your "Thinking Cap"

Your brain has many important jobs, and you are the boss of your brain. The key to boosting your brain power is to choose the thoughts and activities you want to give your attention to. You are constantly rewriting the blueprint for your brain to follow. The daily routines you choose to do and the things you choose to learn are the pathways you will strengthen. Now that you understand how your brain works, you can be better prepared to train your brain to grow and get smarter.

CHAPTER 4

THE POWER OF POSITIVITY

Optimism is having a positive outlook. It also means you are enthusiastic, or excited, about what you are doing or what you have. Optimistic people are hopeful about the future.

You have probably heard that people see a half glass of water as either half full or half empty, depending on whether they are optimistic or pessimistic. If you say it is half empty, you are viewing the situation in a negative (pessimistic) way because you are saying it is closer to gone. If you see it as half full, you are seeing it in a positive way, because you focus on what's there, not what's missing.

Positivity is the practice of having an optimistic attitude. You could think of positivity and negativity like the personalities of vultures and hummingbirds. Vultures seem . . . well, kind of grouchy. They aren't particularly friendly, and they're always in search of rotten things to enjoy. Hummingbirds, on the other hand, appear colorful and cheerful. They flit around looking for sweet things, like nectar, and are drawn to beautiful flowers.

Which personality are you more like? Do you look for the good or the bad in each situation? Maybe you sometimes see more good and sometimes see more bad. Yet few things that happen are totally good or bad. They're mixed. So it is up to *you* to decide how to look at them. Being positive feels good.

Andrew and **Phi** went to a surprise birthday party for their friend, Eleanor. They hung out together at the party and did most of the same things. But when Phi's mom picked them up and asked how it went, they had very different reactions. Andrew said, "The party was great! I got to hang out with some friends I hadn't seen since school got out and the music and dancing were super fun! Oh, and Eleanor was *so* surprised when she walked in! Did you know they got her a puppy? It is adorable!"

Phi didn't agree. "That party was awful," he said. "The food was cold by the time Eleanor got there for the surprise. The house smelled like dog, and the music was so loud you couldn't even talk to each other."

Andrew and Phi were at the same party, yet they had completely different reports. Which person would you rather spend time with? Which person do you think would have more of a growth mindset? Who do you think had more fun?

Being positive isn't just about feeling good and having fun, though. It can be really important when it comes to learning and growing your brain. It's just like choosing to have a growth mindset. Sometimes learning is really hard, and sometimes you'll have setbacks. You can enjoy more success and encourage others to be successful when you choose to have a more positive attitude toward your challenges.

Positive People Persevere

The way you think can change the way you feel. It can affect how you react to failures and successes. Viewing failure in a positive way, as an important part of the process of learning, will help you stay motivated. Viewing failure in a negative way, as a sign you will never understand a skill, may cause you to give up.

When you were little and learning to spell your name, you surely made some mistakes. Maybe you mixed up the letters or wrote one of them backward. Or maybe you left out a letter or two. When that happened, did your parent say, "Well, looks like he'll never be able to read and write. He can't even spell his name." No way! Instead, your family was optimistic. They saw the positive side of you trying. They had confidence that you would keep trying and eventually be able to do it. They probably helped you learn from your mistakes and encouraged you to try again.

Sometimes it's easy to be optimistic when you first start doing something, but your attitude can change when the thing you're doing gets really hard. For example, have you ever participated in a long running or swimming race? In an event like this, you may feel confident at the starting line. But later in the race, you probably start to get tired and sore. At some point, it may be harder to believe that you will finish. That's when being positive really helps! If you have a positive attitude, you are more likely to push through and finish the race even though your body is hurting and you would rather be home taking a shower. A positive attitude can be just as important as hard work and practice in finishing that race.

When things get hard, do you usually keep working, or are you more likely to give up? It might depend on how positive you are feeling that day, or how you feel about the thing you're doing. (Maybe you're pretty positive about running races but not so much about doing a science project!)

Positive Thinking Has Health Benefits

The Mayo Clinic is one of the most respected medical research centers in the United States. A Mayo study showed that there are many health benefits to positive thinking too. Some of them include:

- an increased life span (that's a pretty good benefit!)
- lower rates of depression
- greater resistance to the common cold
- better coping skills in times of stress

How Positive Is Your Attitude?

Just like most people don't have a growth mindset all the time or a fixed mindset all the time, most people aren't typically all positive or all negative. Different situations may cause you to behave in different ways. For example, if you have a headache, you may not be as tolerant of loud noises. So at that time you might avoid going to your brother's room when his music is blaring. It's not because you have a negative attitude about music (or your brother). It's because your headache is preventing you from enjoying the music at the time.

However, many people tend to lean one way or the other. What about you? If you were to ask someone close to you, like a parent or close friend, do you think they would say you are mostly positive? All people go through hard times or have bad days, but for the most part, do you tend to look on the bright side? Take the survey on page 59 to help you decide if you tend to have more of a positive outlook or a negative one. You can print it at freespirit.com/mindset, or just write your answers in your notebook or on your device.

Strategies for Adding Positivity to Your Life

If you've seen the movie *Mary Poppins*, you may remember this famous line from one of her songs: "A spoonful of sugar helps the medicine go down!" In other words, something sweet can make it easier to handle something bitter or harsh. That is a way you can look at being positive. A dose of optimism helps you deal with challenges. Here are six tools you can use to help you be more positive.

Compare Yourself Only to Yourself

One of the most important ways to build optimism and an enthusiasm for pursuing greatness is to avoid comparing yourself to others. That can sometimes be a real joy killer.

How Positive Is Your Attitude?

Read each scenario and decide where you stand in each example.

1 = Nope   2 = Sometimes   3 = Usually   4 = Yesssss!

_____ **1.** I wake up excited to start my day and can't wait to see what great things will happen.

_____ **2.** I can turn any bad situation into a better situation by looking at the bright side.

_____ **3.** People often describe me as a positive person.

_____ **4.** I'm usually able to cheer up someone who is grumpy or sad.

_____ **5.** I look for opportunities to encourage others to be positive.

_____ **6.** When something I try doesn't work, I am thankful for the lesson and try again.

_____ **7.** If someone puts me down, I don't take it personally.

_____ **8.** When I don't meet a goal, I set a new one and look forward to the feeling I will experience when I do meet it.

_____ **9.** When there is bad news, I watch for the good that comes of the situation.

_____ **10.** I enjoy figuring out what I can learn from a mistake.

Add up all your answers and compare the final number to the scores on the next page. How positive is your attitude?

→

How Positive Is Your Attitude? continued

If you scored 35–40
Wow, you are extremely positive! Keep spreading good vibes.

If you scored 23–34
Way to go—you are positive and balanced! You are able to see the bright side and maintain good thoughts in tough situations.

If you scored 22 or below
You may have some negative tendencies, which can keep you from going after your goals or encouraging someone else to work toward their own. But there's good news! You can try some of the strategies in this chapter to give your positive vibes a boost.

Your score on this survey can help you better understand your everyday outlook. No matter what your score is, you can choose to change your thinking. Everyone can! Looking for ways to be more positive can help you feel better about yourself and enjoy life more. It can even help you achieve your goals and be more successful!

Think of it this way: What you see someone else doing at one particular place and time does not show you how much effort they put in ahead of time. A skill that may appear to have come easily could have taken years of hard work and practice. But all you see is the finished product, so it might *seem* like things come easier for the other person than they do for you.

Faye bounced into the classroom, grinning from ear to ear. She ran up to her friend, **Cadence**, and put her hands on both her shoulders. "Guess what!" Faye said. "I got the part in the play!"

Cadence smiled back and said, "Nice! That's great."

Cadence was happy for her friend, but for some reason, she started to feel a little blue. She didn't understand it. After all, she didn't want to be in the play and didn't try out. Faye getting the part didn't take anything away from Cadence.

That evening at dinner, Cadence's mom brought up the play. "Faye must be so excited! Let's get tickets as soon as they go on sale."

"Yeah, sure. That will be fun," Cadence said unconvincingly.

Her mom picked up on her tone. "You know, Faye worked really hard learning lines and practicing the audition dance. Her mom said she spent hours each night to get it just right."

"I know," Cadence said. She thought for a second and added, "I guess I'm a little jealous. I wish I had something I was really good at like that. Something that people got excited about."

"What about the bracelets you made this week? You've been working hard on your jewelry making."

"Yeah, so? That's not as great as being the lead in the school play."

"Maybe not yet," her mom said. "But do you remember the first bracelets you made last summer?"

"How could I forget?" Cadence said. "They were *not* good."

"You were just beginning. But you kept working and getting better. Look how far you've come. You can be proud of that."

Cadence's face brightened. "I have really gotten better, haven't I?"

"Definitely," her mom said.

The next day at school, Cadence handed a box to Faye. "I'm sorry if I didn't seem too excited about your news. Here is a good luck charm for you as you get ready for the play. I can't wait to watch you next month on the stage!"

Faye opened the box and put on the new bracelet right away. "You made this? Wow, I love it! Thank you so much!"

It can be hard to see other kids experience success in sports or clubs or with their grades when you feel like you aren't doing as well. However, it's important to remember that you are learning and practicing at different paces and on different skills. You have things you're really good at, and there are things you haven't even tried yet.

If you compare yourself to *you*, and appreciate *your* progress, comparison can bring you joy. Imagine you are on a swim team. Most of the other kids on the team are faster than you, so you're not very optimistic about how you're going to perform at meets. Instead of feeling bad about how you compare to the other swimmers, you can shift your thinking. Concentrate on comparing your new time to your old time. If you improve, then that is progress—and something to be proud of! First-place ribbons are nice, but so is doing your own personal best.

Everyone learns things at different times and with different tools and efforts. Some people need many repetitions to learn, while others catch on with fewer. Think about popcorn. All of the kernels go into the same popper, with the same heat and the same oil. But they never all pop at the same time. Be patient and keep building up positive energy. Your chance to pop will come if you believe in yourself.

Find Positive People

One way to boost your attitude in a positive way is to hang around positive people. Attitudes are contagious. Have you ever been in a group of people complaining and caught yourself joining in with the complaints and negative energy? On the other hand, have you ever felt your energy level go up when you're around people who seem genuinely happy? These people light up a room and bring a smile to your face. You want to be around them.

One great way to add more positivity to your life is to seek out people who are usually positive. Do you have a friend who loves to make jokes? Or is always willing to try something new? Or who believes in you and gives you positive encouragement? Is there a family member you can rely on to cheer you up when you need it, or who gets excited to share a funny video or story with you, or who always seems to look on the bright side of things? Those are people you may want to spend more time with. They make life better.

At the same time, if someone in your life is negative *most* of the time, this could be bringing you down. Can you have a chat with the person about how that makes you feel? Maybe you can help add some positive energy to your relationship. If the person doesn't change, try not to take their negative comments personally. You may want to hang out with that person less often, if possible.

The people in your life—at home, at school, and in your community—will experience a range of emotions. (Just like *you* experience a range of emotions.) You can't always be surrounded by positivity. As much as you'd like to, even *you* won't feel like being positive all the time. If you are feeling sad about something, that's okay. You don't have to fake being happy. Sometimes things really are lousy. This might be a great time to seek out one of those people who are reliably positive. Give the person a call or text, or see if you can get together. Even if you're just feeling down and you're not sure why, a positive pal who cares about you can listen, and might help you break out of your rut.

You can do the same thing for others. Showing kindness is a way to be positive. Sometimes people have a bad day or are dealing with a hard situation that you don't know about. When a person you know is struggling to be positive, you can try to spread kindness to brighten their day, offer to be a listening ear, or ask if you can help in some way. You could say:

" **Looks like you're having a rough day.** " **I'm sorry. Want to talk about it?**

" **I know what it's like to be in a bad mood.** " **What would help you feel better?** **Do you want to ride bikes?**

" **Is there anything I can do for you?** " **I'm here for you if you need help.**

People are kind of like power plants. Power plants take energy from one source, like the sun or the wind, and transfer it somewhere else, like your home. As a human, you take *emotions* and transfer them to those around you. You can spread happiness and gratitude, or anger and bitterness. This is a big deal because you are responsible for the energy you project into the world. Choose your attitudes carefully. Choose to be a joy generator!

Seek Out People Who'll Support You

When you're in the thick of trying something that really pushes you, and you're feeling uncomfortable or anxious, you can get a huge boost from peers and mentors who can cheer you on or remind you of your ability. More than just being positive, these are people who are on your side. They support you.

Who are the people in your life you can turn to when you need a boost? Could you talk to a parent? A teacher? A religious leader or youth group leader? A family member? A friend?

If you are feeling discouraged, you can try some of these conversation starters to get help from someone you trust:

" Can I talk to you " about something I'm trying to do?

" Do you have " some advice for how I can work through this problem?

" I'm stuck and wonder " if you can help me.

" I could use a " cheerleader right now.

" How do you " stay positive when this happens to you?

" Can you help me " with _____?

" What's your " advice when _____ happens?

Reaching out is a great way to learn from a person who may have gone through a similar situation. Even if they haven't, they can help calm you when you feel stressed and encourage you when you need it. Maybe someday you can repay the favor and cheer that person on.

Leading up to the big reading test, fifth-grader **Jamal** was ready. He had worked hard in class and felt optimistic about how he would perform on the test. His teacher had shown them a fun video to get them pumped up and feeling good about doing their best.

The first few questions of the test confirmed his confidence. Jamal knew the answers and kept moving at a comfortable pace. The next section required reading a long poem. He didn't know what some of the words meant, and the questions afterward were confusing. They weren't like questions he had ever seen on a test before. He wasn't quite sure what "analogy" the author was making in the second stanza, or what that even meant.

Suddenly, Jamal began to doubt his ability to understand what he read. He started to look around the room. It seemed like everyone else was doing okay. They were still clicking answers on their screens. Jamal's stomach started to hurt.

Jamal raised his hand and told his teacher he was confused. Mr. Dax asked Jamal what he was having trouble with. Jamal replied honestly, "The questions are different than I'm used to and seem really hard. I read the poem, but I don't understand what some of it means."

Mr. Dax patted his shoulder. "Jamal, it looks like you've reached problems that are above your reading level. That means you must have answered our grade level's questions correctly. The test automatically bumps you up to more difficult questions to see what you can do. It looks like you may have some middle school questions there! Keep up the good work!"

That helped Jamal relax. He felt proud of himself for doing well and was happy he asked for help. Now, focused with a renewed helping of positive thoughts, Jamal finished the rest of the test, doing the best he could.

Teachers can be a great resource when you need support. They know just how to help you learn and encourage you when you need it.

Have an Attitude of Gratitude

Another effective way to be positive is to be mindful of what you are grateful for. If you're feeling bummed out or cranky, that can be hard to do. Some people keep a gratitude journal or list to help them remember to be grateful. You can do that too. Write down things that you're thankful for or that make you feel good. Examples might be:

- People you are grateful for, like those who support you or make you laugh

- Things that happened that were positive, like enjoying a beautiful, sunny day

- Acts of kindness you appreciate, like if someone helped you with a chore or said something nice to you when you needed it

- Opportunities you've been given, like the chance to go on a field trip and learn about a new place

- Beautiful, amazing, or cool things you've observed, from small things like cute baby animals playing together to bigger things like a huge group of people working together for a cause or a great concert you saw

Many people who record what they are thankful for on a daily basis say that they are happier because they are focusing on the goodness in their lives.

Use Positive Self-Talk

When something bad happens, or you just need a little motivation, you can stay positive by telling yourself encouraging thoughts like, *I'm going to learn a ton from this mistake!* Or, *Well, if I'm going to mess up, at least I did it in the biggest way possible!* It's a much better result than being negative and thinking, *Well, there goes that goal.* Or, *I'm such an idiot!*

If you run into an obstacle, stay focused on the result, or the end goal. You can remind yourself, *It's going to feel so good when I reach this goal!* With each step forward, you are improving in some small way. When there are no cheerleaders around, cheer for yourself in your own mind: *I can do this! I've got what it takes! Keep moving forward!*

Make a plan ahead of time to help you deal with doubt and pressure before you start to struggle. When you are in the middle of feeling defeated or have a major setback, it can be hard to come up with positive thoughts to motivate yourself. But if you've practiced some ideas, they will come more easily when you need them. Think of some phrases that could help encourage you when you encounter negative thoughts. Take or draw a picture of yourself, put it in your notebook, and make a speech bubble above you. What could you put in the bubble to tell yourself?

Here are a few ideas:

Pull this out or think of what you wrote the next time you are having a hard time accomplishing something. It could be a physical challenge, like running, or a brain buster, like a hard math problem.

Do a Daily Kindness Challenge

Here is an idea you can try to kick-start each day on a positive note. Think of one act of kindness you can do for someone else. Doing nice things for others makes the world around us a better place, and it can help you feel good about making a positive difference. It could be for a family member, someone at school, a neighbor, or even someone on the other side of the world. It doesn't have to cost anything. Sometimes, just a sincere compliment or making a point to hold the door for someone can make a big difference for another person. You can occasionally do something bigger, like sharing fresh-baked muffins or inviting a classmate who needs a friend to join your recess game.

You could even record your kind acts in a "Daily Deeds" notebook. You will experience such joy when you get in the habit of doing a daily kind act for others.

If you start your day off thinking of kind ways you can make a difference for others and what you are thankful for, your brain gets trained to look for the good. Your brain scans the world for the positive instead of the negative. Your thoughts start to focus on what you have to be thankful for rather than what you don't have.

Being kind and staying focused on joy helps with a growth mindset because you *do* better when you *feel* better. You are more motivated to help others, and you feel better about your life situation. Happiness and positive thinking help you to be your best.

JOT YOUR THOUGHTS

What are some things you are grateful for?

What are acts of kindness you have done for others?

Who are some of the positive role models in your life? What makes you view them that way? How could you be a positive role model for someone else?

CHAPTER 5

SETTING YOUR GOALS

What comes to your mind when you think of goals? Do you think of sports and scoring a goal in soccer or hockey? Do you think of New Year's resolutions people set once a year? Are you a part of a club that has a fundraising goal? Do you think of the goals your teacher sets for your classroom or your principal sets for your school?

In this chapter, you'll focus on your own personal goals. Goals are a big part of growth-mindset thinking. When you have goals, you are working toward something you hope to be able to do or to have. Goals give you a focus and a purpose for learning new skills and behaving in certain ways. They help you form healthy habits that grow your brain—and your success.

If you know what you want to learn, you can train your brain to become smarter in those areas. Before you can do that, though, you need to know where your focus should be.

In the following pages, you'll have a chance to establish one or more goals for yourself and make a plan for achieving them. Use the form on page 76 to start brainstorming goals you're interested in pursuing and narrowing the list down. You can print the form at freespirit.com/mindset or write your answers in your notebook or device.

Ready, SET, Goal!

To make sure you have the best chance for success, make sure your goal includes three important parts. You can use the word SET to help you remember the important components of setting a goal:

S – SPECIFIC TARGET
E – EFFORT STEPS
T – TIMEFRAME

Specific Target

Be sure you are **specific** in your goal so you have a target to aim for. If you just say, "I'll be nicer to my sister," you don't really know what it looks like to meet your goal. Does that mean buying her candy every day? Does it mean giving her compliments? Both of those are pretty nice. To make your goal of being nice more specific, you could say, "I won't raise my voice to my sister." That gives you a **Specific Target** to aim for, and you can measure if you have hit it. If you don't raise your voice to your sister, then you have accomplished your goal (and it doesn't matter if you bought her candy or not).

Goal-Storming

What are some things you'd like to learn? What have you always been interested in or curious about? Is there a skill you'd like to improve on? Check out the four categories below and try to think of some ideas for each one.

For now, your goals can be general or vague, or just starter ideas (like "get better at eating healthy"). You will learn how to make more specific goals—and plans for reaching them—later in this chapter.

1. Sports and Athletics

These goals might be things like scoring a certain number of points in a basketball game, nailing your front tuck in gymnastics, learning a new sport or skill, or challenging yourself to ride your bike a certain number of miles.

2. Creative

Goals in this box might be in areas like music, games, puzzles, crafts, writing, drawing, and so on.

$\longrightarrow$

Goal-Storming continued

3. Academic

These goals are school-related, like beating your time on a fact quiz or improving your spelling test score.

4. Positive Habits

You may set goals for positive habits—things that are important to you for personal growth—like making your bed every day, doing a random act of kindness each week, making new friends, reading more, being on your phone less, and so on.

Now look at all the goals you brainstormed and circle the ones that are most important to you. Choose one goal that you can focus on for this chapter that is going to help you improve in some area of your life. Which goal is it?

Effort Steps

The **Effort Steps** are the things you will need to do in order to achieve the target. (Just like your target, these should be specific too.) Maybe the **Effort Steps** for the goal of not raising your voice to your sister are:

1. Keep myself calm and my voice soft if she starts an argument.

2. If my sister makes a mean face at me, I will smile at her or walk away.

3. If my sister does something to upset me, I'll talk to her about how it feels for me.

Timeframe

The last part of setting a goal is determining your **Timeframe** for meeting it. Sometimes that means how long you will keep doing something (or *not* doing it). You might set the goal of being nice to your sister for a date one month away. You'll know you have met the goal if you used your Effort Steps successfully during the month and didn't yell at your sister. Who knows? Maybe she'll want to buy *you* candy for being so kind!

Sometimes the **Timeframe** measures how long you think it will take to complete something. For example, if your goal is to make a quilt, your **Timeframe** will lay out how often you work on it and for how long. "I will work on my quilt for one hour five nights a week for four weeks." If you don't end up finishing in that time, you may have to add more time.

Put It All Together

Let's try an example of an academic goal. Maybe you need to complete a biography report about a famous scientist.

Specific Target

- I will create a slideshow presentation about Mae Jemison with ten slides and 300 words total by the due date in three weeks.

Effort Steps

- I will read one book and three web resources about Mae Jemison and take notes.

- I will organize the information and create visuals to put on the keynote slides.

- I will practice my presentation in the mirror and in front of someone in the family.

Timeframe

- I will research and take notes on the materials for 30 minutes each night for one week.

- I will organize the information onto the slides and create visuals for 30 minutes each night for the second week.

- I will practice my presentation at least once each night the third week, up until my presentation date.

With all three of these guidelines established for your goal, you are setting yourself up for success.

Salma's teacher, Ms. McCoo, asked her class to write down a goal for the first two weeks of school. Last weekend Salma's dad told her she needed to be more responsible, so she wrote, "Be more responsible."

Zaide was in the middle of a great book and wanted to finish it. He wrote, "Finish the novel I started before September 1st. To do that, I will read for 30 minutes a night and in my free time during the school day."

Hadley struggled with spelling sometimes, so she wrote, "Practice my spelling words every night by writing them two times each and having my dad quiz me out loud. Get at least a 90 percent on my first test."

After two weeks had passed, Ms. McCoo asked the kids to raise their hands if they met their goals. Zaide's and Hadley's hands shot up. Any chance Zaide got, his nose was in his book, devouring every word. He even finished the book a day early. Hadley had practiced her spelling words each night, just as she had planned, and aced the spelling test. They had both accomplished their goals.

Salma wasn't sure. She hadn't forgotten to pack her lunch. Did that mean she was responsible? She did forget to make her bed some days, so maybe she stayed the same? Ms. McCoo came over to her desk to see her goal. "Why don't you know if you met your goal?" she asked.

"I'm not sure how to know if I improved," Salma said.

"Let's try to get more specific," Ms. McCoo said. "In what way do you want to be more responsible?"

Salma rewrote her goal more specifically: "I'll be prepared for school each day."

"Great," Ms. McCoo said. "Now, what Effort Steps can you take to accomplish your goal in the two weeks?"

Salma wrote her steps, "I will be prepared by charging my tablet, packing my lunch, and filling out my reading log every night."

Narrowing down her goal of being more responsible for school and creating specific Effort Steps not only helped Salma stay focused on remembering what she needed to do, but also allowed her to know if she succeeded. The next time Ms. McCoo asked who made their goals, Salma's hand shot up.

Salma had a personal goal—to be more responsible. But until she set up a Specific Target and laid out specific Effort Steps, she had trouble measuring whether she'd accomplished that goal. (Her teacher gave her the Timeframe of two weeks.) Once she had those to use as a guideline, she knew what to shoot for. And after the two-week Timeframe was over, she knew that she hit it.

Take Action on a Goal

Are you ready to make your own goal using SET? Take a look at the goal you chose on the "Goal-Storming" form on pages 76–77. You will use that idea to write out a goal with a plan for accomplishing it.

Print the "My Goal" form on page 83 at freespirit.com/mindset, or write your answers in your notebook or device. As you read through the SET steps on the next pages, fill in your answers on the form.

Naming a Specific Target

Does the goal you chose have a Specific Target? If not, think about how you can give it one. What are the actual results that you want to see? What does success look like exactly? For example, if your goal is to do better in social studies, what does that look like? Do you want to raise your grade? In that case, you can use a particular grade as the Specific Target. Do you want to know more about a certain time in history? Your Specific Target can be to spend a certain amount of time researching about it.

Write down a Specific Target for your goal under "Specific Target" on your "My Goal" sheet.

Creating Effort Steps

Now it's time to look at what Effort Steps will be required to meet your goal. Remember to keep them specific, just like your target. Effort Steps might be specific skills you need to practice or routines you need to go through. They might involve things you need to learn, like strategies or new information. You might even

My Goal

Specific Target

_____

_____

_____

_____

Effort Steps

_____

_____

_____

_____

_____

_____

Timeframe

_____

_____

_____

_____

have getting help from a mentor as one of your steps. Your Effort Steps might be things you need to . . .

- **KNOW**
- **DO**
- **GET**
- or **FIND** to make progress.

For example, if your goal is to win the spelling bee, you would need to practice the words on the list. So one of your steps might simply be to spell words from the spelling list a certain number of times. Or maybe you will have a friend quiz you on the words. Is there an app or website with tips or games that could help? If so, you could make using the app one of your steps.

Take some time to figure out what will be required to achieve your goal. Try to be as specific as possible. Write them in the "Effort Steps" section of your "My Goal" form. This will help you to remember what you need to learn and how to practice.

Setting a Timeframe

Your Timeframe might be one you can plan for yourself or it might be determined for you. The Timeframe for the spelling bee example ends on the date of the event. No matter how much time you put into working on your goal, it is going to end when the spelling bee ends. If your goal is one you're doing on your own, you can figure out your own end point. For example, if your goal is to learn how to ollie a skateboard, you can say you'll work on it for a month, or six weeks, or whatever makes sense to you.

Maybe you want to keep working until you reach your goal, no matter how much time it takes. This is often the case with non-academic goals. For the goal of learning to ollie, you might just say you're going to work on it until you learn that skill. If that's what you're planning with your goal, time is still important. Focus on how much time you will spend each day working on your goal. For example, "I will practice ollying for 15 minutes every day after school."

Now look again at your "My Goal" form. You have a Specific Target for your goal, and you've written down some Effort Steps to get there. You're ready to commit to a Timeframe. How long do you want to give yourself to meet your goal? On your form, write down your Timeframe in the space provided.

Congratulations on setting a Specific Target for your goal, with Effort Steps and a Timeframe for completing it. You are on your way to entering the Success Cycle.

Success Cycle

The good news about having a growth mindset and setting a goal is that you are setting yourself up to make progress. The less-good news is those things don't *guarantee* progress. As you start working on your Effort Steps, you might find that some of them are moving you toward your goal—and some are not.

Most goals follow a cycle. You apply effort, you make progress or fail, you learn from it, and you improve in some way. Then you try again with the new improvement. For example, once you are making progress and learning your spelling words, you may find that the app you've been using doesn't help you very much. So you might drop that Effort Step and try to discover new Effort Steps that *can* help you. Then you try again. It's the same with learning to ollie. Maybe you go out every day after school and work on the trick, but you're not getting any better. You might need to find a new Effort Step. Do you need to ask someone for help? Do you need to watch a video for tips?

This process becomes a cycle, where you begin to *try* the various ways to work on your goal. Sometimes you *fail,* and you use those failures to *learn* and *improve,* then *try* again. As you go through the cycle, you learn what works and what doesn't. In other words, sometimes you don't nail your Effort Steps the first time you write them. It could be that you weren't specific enough, or maybe you need to try a different way to learn or practice. What is this cycle called? You guessed it:

The Success Cycle

Let's say your goal is to learn a song on the keyboard, and you write an Effort Step of practicing it for 20 minutes per night. But you keep forgetting to practice, and you don't make any progress. In order to eventually succeed, you need to learn from that mistake. Maybe you need to adjust your Effort Steps to make your practice time is a little shorter, so you're more likely to sit down and do it. Or maybe you need to set an alarm to remind you when it is time to practice each evening. Those changes could make all the difference in meeting your goal.

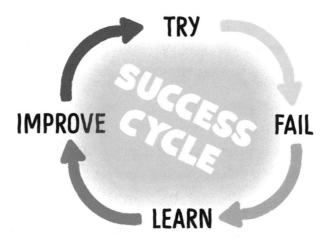

Some goals may be fairly simple, and you will be able to meet them after going through the cycle just once or twice. Other goals are more complex. For some goals, you may have to go through the cycle many times before you finally have success. All goals are unique, and you will learn as you work on them what you need to adjust to improve.

Be a Goal Keeper

Goals come in all shapes and sizes. Some are small and can be accomplished relatively easily. Others are much bigger and require a lot of planning and determination to stick with and achieve. You can think of your goals as falling into one of three categories: short-term, medium-term, and long-term.

Short-Term Goals

These may be goals that you can accomplish in a matter of hours or a day. They might be things you put on a to-do list. Maybe a short-term goal is to get your side of the closet cleaned out. It may still require Effort Steps, like emptying it out, sorting through your things, donating clothes that don't fit, starting a yard-sale pile, and then putting everything back in neatly. But you can get it done without planning too far ahead into the future.

Medium-Term Goals

These goals may take days or weeks. They usually require many more action steps or practices to accomplish. Goals like this could be for learning a new skill or creating a project for school.

Long-Term Goals

These are more of the gargantuan variety. Long-term goals require months or maybe even years to accomplish. Maybe you want to learn how to play an instrument. Perhaps you want to earn a certain kind of scholarship or get a particular job when you are older. Even though it may seem weird to think of something so far away, knowing what you want in life can help guide you to make decisions now that will help you get there.

Most people work on a few different goals at the same time. You may be working on eating healthier as a long-term goal while also working on a short-term goal to finish writing your English essay before bedtime. And maybe you'll add in the medium-term goal of trying to master your table-tennis serve in the next two weeks.

By setting goals and making action plans to achieve them, you can accomplish a lot—in the short-term, medium-term, *and* long-term. It can be exciting and empowering to start thinking about the future. For example, if you think you might want to be a veterinarian someday, you can start down that path now by walking people's dogs, training your pet rabbit to follow an agility course, joining science clubs, and subscribing to podcasts and reading magazines about animals.

It's okay if you haven't thought this far into the future yet. Try it now, or just start thinking about it. Your goals don't have to be final. It is good to consider long-term goals even if they change later. It won't be a waste if you decide down the road that you don't want to be a vet. You learn a lot just by trying things out. With that experience, you'll be able to make more informed decisions about what you do and don't want.

CHAPTER 6

HOCUS POCUS, TIME TO FOCUS

As you work through the success cycle to meet your goal, sometimes it's a challenge to stay focused. It can be easy to stray from the path and not meet your goals if you get distracted, feel frustrated, or forget your purpose.

Your chances of making the volleyball team won't improve if you're just hitting a beach ball over the net and being silly. You have to be deliberate and focused on using your new skills correctly so you get better. Focus is what will keep you improving and on the right track.

Steady as You Go

Staying focused doesn't mean you only think about your one goal all the time. You have to live your life! If your goal is to learn how to serve a table-tennis ball with topspin, you still have to do chores, eat meals, go to school, and do homework. Not to mention play with your pet, spend time with friends, watch movies with your family, and do other things to relax and have fun. You have lots of things to focus on. But if you stay focused on your table-tennis goal, you won't forget to practice every day in the rec center after school. Most goals you can't accomplish all at once. You have to keep your focus over a period of time.

A great example of the power of focus is the old tale of the tortoise and the hare. In this story, the speedy hare challenges the slow-and-steady tortoise to a race. The hare is so sure he will win that he gets distracted, takes breaks, and forgets what his goal is. Meanwhile, the tortoise is focused on finishing the race and just keeps going. Even though the tortoise is slower than the hare, he remains faithful to his goal and keeps taking small steps toward it. In the end, he wins the race.

One reason it's a good idea to write down your goals and make a plan to meet them is that it helps keep your goals in mind as you go about your life. Even when you're doing something unrelated, part of you stays focused on that goal. It stays in the back of your mind because it was important enough for you to plan out. And if you start to slip and lose focus, you can go back and look at your Effort Steps and make changes if you need to.

Ella loves reading graphic novels and enjoys drawing. She decided it would be fun to write one over the summer. She used SET to make her goal become a reality. She started by writing down her Specific Target: "I will write and illustrate my own graphic novel."

Next, Ella figured out her Effort Steps:

1. Read one graphic novel per week for inspiration.

2. Write and illustrate four full pages per week of her own graphic novel.

Her Timeframe was the summer. There are 10 weeks in the summer, so she figured she could have a 40-page book completed by the time school started if she stuck with her plan of completing four pages per week.

Ella was very excited to have this plan in place, and the first few weeks went well. She kept up her pace of reading graphic novels and writing and drawing her own. But then the weather got *really* nice, and the pool at the park started calling her name. She also loved playing kickball with her friends in the evenings and going for walks. Just like her graphic novel, all those things were important to her. But with so much going on, Ella lost her focus on her goal and went a week without writing or illustrating a single page. Then her family went on a week-long vacation. Uh-oh.

By the time she returned from vacation, Ella was eight pages behind on her Effort Step of working on her book. But she never forgot about it, and she wasn't ready to give up. She decided she needed to revise her plan to keep focused and catch up. She bumped the number of pages she had to do each week to five, and she made an important addition to her Effort Step: she would work on her pages in the morning before breakfast each day. This would allow her to fully focus, first thing in the morning, and still have the rest of the day to enjoy time with her friends in the lovely weather.

This time, Ella stuck to her goal. As she made progress, she was even more determined to stick with her plan. For a couple of weeks, she completed six pages instead of five because she got on a roll and didn't want to stop.

By the end of the summer, Ella had finished the book! It was a challenging process, but now she had a new skill, doing something she enjoyed. And there was a bonus: when school started up again, she realized she had learned a lot about managing a big project, and she'd improved her reading and writing skills. This helped her do even better on school projects. All of that thinking about stories paid off!

Ella got distracted by all the fun and freedom that summer has to offer. Hey, sometimes that happens! But her goal was important enough to her that she was able to go back and find her focus again, making some changes in order to help her *keep* her focus.

Did you notice another good thing that happened to Ella? Working on her graphic novel was a personal goal—just for her—but it helped her in school too. That's another benefit of making goals and making plans to achieve them. Your focus and hard work in one area can rub off in other areas of your life.

Imagine that your goal is to cut down on sugar because you had a bad checkup at the dentist. As you work on the goal, you may notice that your energy level is more even. You are able to focus better in class. You set that goal to help your teeth, but it helped you with mental alertness at school too. Or you might set a goal to learn how to prepare healthy meals. If you start helping your mom cook, you could enjoy other bonuses besides good food and cooking skills. For example, all that practice measuring ingredients may help you understand math fractions better. You may also create a stronger bond with your mom as you learn new recipes together. That's a triple bonus!

Ways to Keep Your Focus

Okay, so focus is important. But sometimes it's hard. You need some strategies to help you—hey, did your phone just buzz? Don't look! Stay focused! Here are a few helpful tips and tools that can make it easier to focus like a laser—zzzzzap!—on your goal.

Keep Your Eye on the Why

One of the best ways to keep your focus is to remind yourself *why* you're doing what you're doing. Is it so you can get better at a skill that is important to you? Is it to challenge yourself and see what you are capable of? Is it to help someone in need? If you understand and care about why you are working so hard, you are more likely to keep working. That's because your *purpose* usually feels more important than any specific outcome.

If you want to get an A on a test, think about *why* that is important to you. Sure, part of it might be to see that letter "A" written on the top of the page. More than likely, though, your purpose is deeper than that. You care because you want to prove to yourself that you can do it. Or you want to show your parents or teacher that you worked hard and deserve it. Or you want to build skills that you can use in the future in class and in life. Whatever the reason for caring about doing your best on the test, it will motivate you to focus on making that happen. Keep your purpose in the back of your mind—or in the front of your mind! You will feel good when you study because it will reinforce what you know you want to accomplish.

Sometimes it's easier to think about the *why* by picturing the outcome of your goal. What will the benefit be? If you can clearly visualize how good it will feel to accomplish what you are working on, you are more likely to keep going to experience that feeling. Actually close your eyes and imagine it. Make an image in your mind with lots of details—sights, sounds, smells, and more.

For example, if your goal is to spin your table-tennis serve, what will it look like as the ball touches down on the far side of the table and glances at an angle, fooling your opponent? (Imagine your opponent too! Maybe it's your brother, and he swings and misses at your awesome serve. *Yes!*) What will it sound like when the ball pops off your paddle and hits the table? What will it feel like in your muscles to have that kind of control over the ball?

Take Breaks

It's good to work hard at goals, but if you push yourself too hard for too long, your ability to do a good job will not stay at its peak. In other words, too much focus can lead to less focus. To prevent that from happening, you may need to take breaks. Be careful, though. That doesn't mean you should quit studying history and get wrapped up playing with the cat for two hours! Make sure your breaks are short so you can get back to work and finish the job. It doesn't take long to refresh your focus and your attitude.

Have you ever had a smartphone or computer freeze on you? If you have, you probably know about the most common way to fix a frazzled machine: turn it off and turn it back on again. This can wipe away whatever was tangling those circuits and give the device a fresh start. The same can be true for humans! Sometimes you need to let your mind reset so you can get back to doing your best work. That's why many teachers take "brain breaks" in their classrooms. When you've been working hard on a skill or are in your seat for an extended period of time, you need to get up and moving to reset yourself.

Doing something physical like jumping jacks, a short walk, or a few push-ups can give your mind the rest it needs and get more blood pumping to your brain. Even just getting up and stretching at your desk can give a big boost.

What else can you do on your break?

- Call a friend and say hi. Ask what they are doing and make a plan to get together later. It feels good to connect with others, and you'll have something to look forward to.

- Read a few pages in a book. Getting lost in an imaginary world can help you get a fresh perspective on your real world.

- Do a mindfulness activity of some kind, like deep breathing or yoga poses.

- Give your pet some scratches or belly rubs, or play a game with it.

- Fix yourself a little healthy snack. Food is fuel for your body and brain.

If you have a long book you're assigned to read, a big report to write, a project you're trying to finish, or anything else that takes a lot of time, you can take more than one break. To make sure these are just short brain breaks to refresh your thinking, set a timer to keep them at five minutes or less. You can also set a timer for how long you will work until you take a break. This gives you something to look forward to—and breaking up the task into chunks like that will help make it feel less overwhelming.

How long can you focus on a task? If you were studying for a science test, do you think you would do well with 15-minute study sessions? You'll have to try it to see. What works for someone else may not be what is the best for you.

Make a To-Don't List

If you are learning to ride a scooter, you don't need to study the history of transportation or know who invented the scooter. You don't need to know the name of every part of the scooter. You *do* need to know how to stand on it and push. You need to learn how to steer and keep your balance. You need to know how to use the brakes. If you are studying the wrong things, you won't make progress.

Of course, that's a bit of a silly example. If you are learning to ride a scooter, you are probably not going to be distracted by who invented the scooter. The problem with focusing on the right things usually comes when the wrong ones *are* tempting. For example, if your goal is to knit scarves for your brother and sister before winter break, you want to make sure you work for a certain amount every day, and *not* lie on the couch watching videos instead. Or if your goal is to get in shape for hockey season, you want to make sure you're eating healthy, and *not* eating greasy or sugary foods.

Many people try to stay on task by making a to-do list, but have you ever thought about making a *to-don't* list? At the top of your list, write down what you want to accomplish. Under that, write "DON'T." You can write it in big, block letters. Then write down all the things you can think of that might cause a problem with accomplishing your goal. These are the things you want to avoid. If your goal is to make more friends at school, you might put "Don't tease anyone" and "Don't belch in the cafeteria" on your to-don't list. If your goal is to finish the assigned reading for class—and you'd rather be reading about dinosaurs—you might write "Don't get distracted by dinosaur books" on your list.

What could you put on a to-don't list that is keeping you from making your best progress?

Avoid Paralysis by Analysis

Paralysis means you are stuck or have lost the ability to move. *Analysis* means examining something closely. What do you think *paralysis by analysis* could mean in terms of not meeting your goals?

Jack loved math. He enjoyed breaking down problems, thinking about how to approach them, and solving them. He checked his work, and most of the time he arrived at the correct answer.

However, when Jack got a writing assignment, he froze. Math problems usually had a clear path to the right answer. He could use different strategies to solve them, but the answer was either right or wrong. He had the ability to check it and know. But with writing, there wasn't a clear path or correct answer. It required creativity and expression. It could take shape in many different ways.

Having so many options stressed Jack out. When he got a writing assignment, he stared at the blank page anxiously. He composed the opening sentence over and over in his head but was never satisfied. He never felt like it was "right." He got so worried about his writing being imperfect that he didn't produce anything at all. He told his teacher, Mr. Moore, "I'm just not good at writing."

Mr. Moore helped him set a goal to write three sentences. He promised to give Jack feedback right away so he could learn what was working and what wasn't. Jack still felt nervous about putting something down that wasn't perfect. But with Mr. Moore's encouragement, he gave it a try.

After Jack wrote his three sentences, his teacher talked to him about his work, as promised. Mr. Moore helped him figure out what he did well. "You backed up your opinion with a reason," Mr. Moore said. "That's great." He also showed Jack where he could do better. "See this sentence? You could add a couple more details to make your point stronger."

Mr. Moore's advice made sense to Jack, and he revised his sentences to make them stronger. And he decided to set a goal to write four sentences next time, which Mr. Moore promised to respond to. These small and steady steps boosted his confidence and helped him with his anxiety about writing.

Jack became overwhelmed with the seemingly unlimited possibilities for what he could write. He was unable to focus when he couldn't find one correct way to tackle the assignment. His teacher helped him get started by encouraging Jack to break it into small chunks. If he could focus on just a small portion, he wouldn't have to feel like it was such a big task.

If you feel paralyzed by a project or task that seems too big or too hard, try to break it down into smaller "bites." Sometimes looking at the big picture can be intimidating, so just look at what you can do right now. As the saying goes, "A journey of a thousand miles begins with a single step." Think of the tortoise, and keep moving slowly and steadily.

JOT YOUR THOUGHTS

Can you think of an area where you have experienced paralysis by analysis? Why do you think you felt paralyzed?

What could you do to be more fully focused?

CHAPTER 7

DESTINATION: DETERMINATION

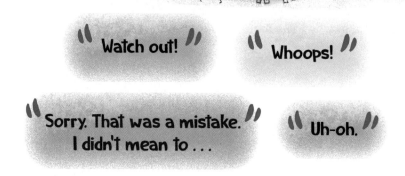

Yes, it's true. Everyone makes mistakes. Not only that, everyone runs into tough times and faces frustrating setbacks. Everyone.

Back in chapter 2 you read that setbacks don't have to hold you back. In fact, a setback can be a set-UP for success. And it's true.

You can do amazing things if you set your mind to it. The key is to be determined. That means you keep striving toward your goal, even when you mess up or it seems hard or you start to lose your motivation. This chapter is all about hanging in there when things get tough—why this matters, and how to do it.

Stick to It to Do It

Most things that are worth doing are not easy. If you want to be a great rapper, you have to write lots of rhymes and practice a lot. If you want to be an amazing wide receiver, you have to run lots of routes and catch lots of footballs. You work hard, and keep working hard. You don't give up. That's determination.

When you first open the box of a 1,000-piece puzzle, you may feel overwhelmed. It might seem hard to get to work when there's so much to do. But soon you start fitting together some pieces. You form a corner and part of a border. Then you complete the frame, and then more and more of the inside. As you figure it out, piece by piece, you start to see the big picture. How satisfying is it when you finally get to place that final piece into the remaining empty spot? Doesn't that feel awesome? It's all because you were determined to finish and kept working.

The Fruits of Failure

Many successful people had to deal with mistakes and failures before they found that success. Dr. Seuss, as you know, was very famous and wrote many fun books. People still celebrate his birthday every year on Read Across America Day. But Dr. Seuss's first book was rejected 27 times by publishers before one finally said yes. He believed in his story, *And to Think That I Saw It on Mulberry Street,* and he was determined to get it published.

Dr. Seuss is just one example. Think about these other "famous failures":

- Oprah Winfrey was once fired from her job as a news reporter, and told that she let her emotions get in the way of reporting. Did Oprah give up? No! She went on to host her own TV show, create a TV network, and much more.

- One of Walt Disney's first newspaper editors fired him for not being creative enough. Yet Disney believed in himself and kept working, creating memorable characters like Mickey Mouse and winning 22 Academy Awards.

- Gymnast Simone Biles didn't make the US junior national team—yet she kept training and has won a combined total of 30 Olympic and World Championship medals.

Imagine if Dr. Seuss, Oprah Winfrey, Walt Disney, or Simone Biles had let their failures stop them! Hard work, determination, and a focus on the goal can keep you from sliding into feeling powerless over your future.

Knowing that these accomplished people have had to deal with rejection helps us remember that failure is, many times, a part of the process. As Oprah Winfrey said, "Failure is another steppingstone to greatness."

There are many reasons people may not do the work necessary to accomplish a goal. Sometimes they don't know what the right work is. Sometimes they know what to do but are afraid of failing. Sometimes they come up with excuses for why they can't handle doing the work. Maybe it seems like all the mistakes they might make could never add up to enough learning to overcome their obstacles.

One thing is for sure, though. Everyone can work hard, stay determined, and keep trying. When you do, your efforts and time will pay off!

JOT YOUR THOUGHTS

What is one brave thing you can do to take a step toward achieving your goals? Is anything holding you back? How can you keep your focus on the goal, rather than your setbacks?

The Magic of Mistakes

When someone grows taller in a short amount of time, people sometimes call that a "growth spurt." You could say the same thing about mistakes. When you make a mistake while trying something new, you learn more and grow your brain quicker than if you had done it right the first time. Mistakes cause your brain to work harder, so your learning is deeper and lasts longer.

You can look at the word **FAIL** differently too. Try thinking of it this way:

F – First
A – Attempt
I – In
L – Learning

Think about this. Do you know *anyone* who has experienced only successes and no setbacks or mistakes? As a matter of fact, the most successful people use their mistakes to learn and get better. That's why . . .

Mistakes should be expected, inspected, and respected!

What do you think this means? Let's break it down:

- **Mistakes are expected:** Mistakes are gonna happen! Try not to be surprised, feel let down, or be too hard on yourself when they do.

- **Mistakes are inspected:** You can look at why they happened—and you can learn from that.

- **Mistakes are respected:** You can appreciate what you learn from mistakes and use that learning to make improvements and try again. In this way, you respect the process of making mistakes.

You may have heard the saying, "If at first you don't succeed, try, try, again." This is a good encouragement. However, Kid President has another version of this quote that may be even better: "If at first you don't succeed . . . you're normal!"

That's right. Most people try things many times before they finally get them right.

Obviously, talented musicians, athletes, actors, artists, and authors weren't born able to do the things they can do now. They learned each skill with lots of practice, effort, mistakes, and time. Have you ever seen a baby hit a home run or knit a blanket?

Comedian and talk show host Ellen DeGeneres says, "When you take risks, you learn that there will be times when you succeed and times when you fail, and both are equally important." That means you can do well and feel good about it, but you can also mess up and feel just as good about it because it will help you in the long run.

SOMETHING TO TRY

Make a short list of people you know who you admire. You could include relatives, teachers, friends, or religious leaders. Maybe you want to add a coach or musician you know.

Ask one or more of these people if you can interview them about their failures and successes. In what ways did they fail? What mistakes can they tell you about? What did they do after those failures and mistakes?

The Magic of YOU

You are proof that staying determined through setbacks pays off. You may not have 30 championship medals like Simone Biles, and you might not be the host of a hugely popular TV show like Ellen DeGeneres or Oprah Winfrey. But you have done some pretty great things after failing at first.

For example, did you learn how to ride a bike? You surely didn't hop on the first time and ride away! You may have started with training wheels. You wobbled and swerved and slowly got more confident. When you took the training wheels off, you probably crashed—more than once—before you were able to ride very far. You practiced, you wobbled some more, you started and re-started. You didn't give up.

It took a lot of work to train your brain and body to balance and coordinate while in motion. Now that your brain has made those connections, you don't even have to think about how to balance. You just get on and start pedaling. Remember the neural pathways you learned about on pages 38–40? You have made your "biking" neural pathway.

You go through this learning process all the time. Have you ever thrown a Frisbee? It's a tough skill in the beginning. The first time you try it, the disc usually veers off in a weird direction and crashes to the ground before it reaches the other person. Right away, though, your brain starts analyzing what happened and starts making adjustments. Maybe you didn't throw it hard enough or flick your wrist enough. Maybe you didn't aim correctly. You might not even think about this analysis much—it happens automatically.

So you make adjustments and try again a different way. Maybe this time you get it far enough, but it curves off the other direction. Now your brain analyzes this mistake and helps you adjust your throw again. Try not to tilt your hand so much, or try to release it sooner. Even though some of this analyzing happens automatically, you can help the process along by consciously thinking about improving and taking in the information you are learning from each throw. Soon, as you keep adjusting your strategy, you start to get the Frisbee closer to your target.

Here is one more example. Think about the game 20 Questions. In this game, one person thinks about an object. Everyone else tries to figure out what the mystery object is by taking turns asking questions that can be answered with a yes or a no. They are limited to a total of 20 questions. To find the answer, you have to go through a process of gathering information. You don't start out with question number one being a guess: "Is it a candle?" Instead, you might start by asking, "Is it bigger than a shoebox?" Once you have the answer to that, you might ask if it is in the category of food.

Each question gives you an answer that helps you categorize the object and analyze what it might be. If the person says "No, it's not bigger than a shoebox," that tells you something. If the person says "No, it's not food," that tells you even more. Keep asking questions to get more information. Eventually you will find out what it is. But it takes lots of tries to answer correctly.

This game is just like the learning process. No one would expect you to learn a new skill on the first try if you've rarely or never done it before. You have to get information and experience little by little. Once you put all the pieces of information together, though, you start to make those connections and you learn enough to do something really well.

Fear of Failure

If mistakes are so great, why are we so worried about making them sometimes? Chances are, when you were little, you weren't. If you walked into a preschool or kindergarten class right now and asked a question, you would probably see nearly every hand go up in the air to try to answer. Kids that age are not usually worried about being wrong. If you asked them to draw a picture and share it with the group, most would want to do that, and proudly. You could even ask for a volunteer to sing a song alone in front of everyone, and many students would probably be willing. Young kids tend to care more about learning and exploring than other people's opinions of them.

But if you were to go into a fifth- or sixth-grade room and ask a question, fewer hands would go up. Ask sixth graders to draw a picture and they may do that, but they might *not* be willing to show anyone. Ask them to sing a solo, and you might not get any volunteers.

What happens between preschool and upper elementary or middle school? Maybe at some point you tried something hard and couldn't do it, and someone laughed. Or maybe you answered a question in class incorrectly, then a classmate gave the right answer, and you felt bad about it. Maybe you got a low grade in a subject that you loved, and it hurt.

Lots of small things like this happen to kids, and they start to add up. After a while, to protect themselves, people become less willing to try new things in front of others. Or they become less willing to ask questions or show their creations to others. Over time, it starts to feel safer to avoid possible embarrassment or judgment instead of taking chances on trying things.

Fear can hold you back from your goals and from learning what you need to learn. To succeed, **your desire for success needs to be greater than your fear of failure**. You have to stay determined to make progress—even when it seems scary.

Using Failure to Develop YOU

When you fail or make a mistake, you can let that setback **define** you, **diminish** you, or **develop** you. You can choose your reaction when you struggle. Only one of those three will help you have a growth mindset and help you succeed. Can you guess which it is?

define: to determine the meaning of

diminish: to make or become less

develop: to grow or become more advanced

Imagine you are drawing a picture, and you don't like the way it turns out. It's disappointing and frustrating. How will you react?

You can use it to **define** you by thinking, *I can't draw*. (This is fixed-mindset thinking because you believe that your mistake defines how you will always perform.)

OR

You can use the experience to **diminish** you and think, *I have no business holding this pencil or being in this art class. Everyone else is better than I am.* (This is fixed-mindset thinking because you believe that people will always be ahead of you and you will always be less, or worse.)

OR

You can use it to **develop** you: *My pencil has an eraser for a reason. I'll watch the demonstration one more time and then try again.* (This is growth-mindset thinking because you believe that you can grow and get better as you keep trying.)

Sometimes these thoughts come quickly, and you have to pause and recognize what you are feeling. Do you notice you are using *diminishing* or *defining* thoughts? Then try to turn your fixed mindset off, and your growth mindset on, by using *developing* thoughts. Switching your reaction from a negative one to a positive one will help you keep trying. It will help you develop your skills and strengthen your growth-mindset power.

Bryan often knew the answers before others and blurted them out in class. He also tended to take over when he had to be a part of a teamwork activity. For that reason, he was usually picked last for group projects and partner work. On Friday, he heard a classmate call him "Bossy Bryan." Another student said he was a "know-it-all."

That night, his brother noticed he seemed down in the dumps. "What's wrong?" Jake asked.

"I don't have any friends," Bryan said. "They call me bossy, and no one wants to work with me at school. I'm not any fun to be around."

"What?" Jake said. "You have friends. What about Tim, next door? And you just played basketball with Antonio last night at the park."

Bryan had to admit that was true. "But it doesn't change the fact that kids at school think I'm a know-it-all."

"Well, you *are* a smart kid," Jake said. "Maybe not as smart as your big brother. Ha! It's not nice for those kids to call you names, but is there any truth to what they're saying?"

"Are you trying to make me feel worse?" Bryan asked.

"No way," Jake said. "But maybe this is a chance for you to develop yourself. People might appreciate your ideas if they're helpful. They'll *want* to have you as a partner if you're a good problem-solver and if you're kind. Think about basketball. Other kids on the team love it when their teammates have great skills, but not if it means they steal the ball all the time and try to make every shot to get the glory. Everyone has to learn how to be a team player and work together to be successful."

Bryan thought about all of this. It was true that people who steal the ball all the time are annoying. Maybe he could try Jake's advice at school next week. He set a goal to practice self-control and be a good team member in the classroom when answering questions and working in groups.

He settled on three Effort Steps:

1. Raise his hand to answer questions in class. (No blurting answers.)

2. Allow other classmates to share ideas in small groups. (Only share one helpful suggestion after everyone else has a chance to share or if he is directly asked.)

3. Give at least two compliments a day to other students in his class for good ideas or answers.

Bryan decided he would start on Monday, when he returned to school. His timeline would be the whole school year.

Bryan was excited to put his plan into action. The first week was pretty hard, especially resisting the urge to blurt. But his classmates started to notice a difference in his actions and attitude. The following Monday, when it was time to choose partners, Ruby asked him if he wanted to work with her. He happily agreed.

At first, when Bryan said he wasn't any fun to be around, he let his classmates' comments **define** who he was as a person. He let their hurtful words **diminish** his feelings about his abilities. But with his brother's encouragement, Bryan figured out a way to use those kids' comments to **develop** his social skills. He used determination and a growth mindset. He knew he could work hard to be a better classmate and friend in school and applied specific Effort Steps to accomplish that goal.

Strategies for Sticking to It

If you have determination, you have a stick-to-it attitude. (Some people call this *grit*.) You have a willingness to keep trying, even when it is hard or the excitement has worn off. Sometimes you may start off with the best intentions and think you will stick with it, but as soon as the process gets tough or boring, you decide to quit.

No doubt, being determined can be hard sometimes. If it were easy, you wouldn't have to be determined! Here are some strategies you can use to boost your determination.

Remember Your Brain

One way you can keep pushing forward is by reminding yourself that your brain grows and gets stronger pathways as you keep trying.

Your neurons also process information faster, making tasks easier as you practice them. When you find yourself struggling, step back for a second and visualize your brain. Imagine those neurons firing and making stronger paths. You might even want to try something new or extra hard just so you can boost your brain power!

Use Positive Self-Talk

An example of determination can be found in the story of *The Little Engine That Could*. In an attempt to deliver toys, a little train engine uses the powerful traits of optimism *and* determination to muster enough energy to get up a hill. To give herself a boost, she repeats this phrase to herself over and over: "I think I can, I think I can . . ." With those positive thoughts, she keeps going and eventually succeeds.

You can use positive self-talk too. Give yourself a little pep talk with positive, encouraging words. If you are running a race, you can tell yourself to keep putting one foot in front of the other. If you are trying to build a model plane and the instructions seem never-ending, you can tell yourself, "One step at a time." When you are trying to improve a skill for a sport, an instrument, or an academic area, tell yourself, "In some small way, better every day."

Here are some more positive self-talk phrases you can use.

"This is really hard, but it's going to feel awesome when I finish!"

"I'm proud of my progress."

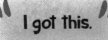

"I'm growing my brain with all this practice."

Beware of Negative "What-If" Thinking

When you're working on a goal and your determination starts to fade, it can be easy to slip into negative "what-if" thinking. For example:

- What if I fail?
- What if they laugh?
- What if I come in last place?

Try to spin those thoughts around into positive what-if thoughts:

- What if I do really well?
- What if everyone loves it?
- What if I win?

Be a Beginner

An important part of determination is confidence. When you believe you can achieve, you have a better chance of sticking to your goals.

One way to build confidence is to be a beginner. This can remind you how it feels to get out of your comfort zone, make a mistake, and remember that it is perfectly okay and normal to do so. You can do this by taking lessons or a class of some kind, or you can also try it on your own.

For example, let's say you've never done ceramics before and you have a chance to take a ceramics class after school. No one will expect you to make a perfect bowl the first time you touch clay. You will need to learn how to prepare the clay, all the techniques for shaping and spinning, and more. You will be in a position where failing is low-risk because it is obvious to everyone that you're starting from the beginning. No one is going to care, or even notice, if your first bowl is crooked or has a leak. What is the worst thing that could happen if your bowl doesn't turn out well? You can learn with confidence, knowing there is nothing to lose.

Doing this can help you remember what it's like to explore and learn new things without fear of failure. It can feel great to be freed up like that, and you may be able to transfer that confident feeling to other things you want to learn.

Ask a parent or another trusted adult to help you find an inexpensive community education class in a skill or topic you're curious about. Or ask someone you know who's really good at it to teach you. You could try writing in cursive, juggling, magic tricks, printmaking, woodworking, inline skating, pottery, quilting, web design . . . the possibilities are endless. Plus, you might love the new thing you try. Maybe you'll be great at it!

Find Help

Finding a mentor, teacher, or coach is a great way to get help when you start to lose your determination. A parent might be able to help you with the project or skill you're working on, or find someone to give you lessons. Maybe a classmate or sibling is just a few steps ahead of you on your goal. Ask that person for some pointers. You don't necessarily have to work with a helper in person, either. You may be able to find a lesson online for the skill or project.

You might not even need a person who knows about the topic. Occasionally you just need someone to talk to and keep you going—someone to say, "You can do it!"

Let's say you want to learn to knit. You could watch video lessons to learn beginning steps. Then you could find a knitting club or a relative who can watch and guide you. Gradually, you will get the feel for making the stitches correctly. Before you know it, you may be able to make all kinds of things out of yarn. You may even decide to learn how to crochet next.

Be Flexible

Being determined does *not* mean you never change your plan or never listen to advice. One of the most powerful qualities determined people have is **flexibility**. This is the ability to adjust and adapt when needed. It means you are able  to change your approach if your original way doesn't work. It's a great growth-mindset skill because it gives you the chance to keep trying, even when things don't work out the way you planned.

Being flexible comes naturally to some people, but others find it tough to shift their approach to the thing they've been working on. Anyone can learn to be more flexible. Just follow these simple steps. Pretty soon flexing your outlook or method will be as natural as touching your toes!

1. Look at what you've learned.

Failure gives you information. When you make a mistake or come up short, ask yourself, "What happened? What can this teach me?" Think about what you can change in order to find a new approach. Look at what has worked and not worked so far to help you figure it out. Do you need more time? More practice? More information? Different tools? By analyzing exactly why you came up short, you can figure out what you need to do differently.

2. Try some new ideas.

Being flexible is all about being open to new ideas. Making mistakes is good, but you want to be making *new* mistakes most of the time. If you keep making the same mistakes, you aren't adapting and learning from them. And you will get the same results. This is your chance to be creative. Look at what you learned about what went wrong, and make changes. If you need more time, think about when you can find it. If you need more information, think about where you can get it. And if you need to try a whole new approach, problem-solve a way to do it.

If you can develop your ability to be more flexible, through creativity and problem-solving, and you are willing to go in new directions, you will find more solutions and paths to your goals.

Faudumo was so excited to begin working on her group's skit. Two of her friends, Kate and Alaina, were in her group, and they all agreed on how they would present their skit. They had a plan for who would prepare and say each part. And they had the whole week to work in class during writing time.

Over the first couple days, the girls got more excited about their presentation. Kate planned to make props. Alaina planned to draw a background scene. And Fadumo planned to record their skit on a tablet.

"Our skit is going to be the best!" said Alaina.

But on Wednesday, everything changed. The girls were setting up their props for their first practice run-through when Mrs. Craig approached their table. "Girls, this is Alberto. It's his first day at our school. I'm adding him to your group because I know you will make him feel welcome. He's still learning English, so he'll want you to help him with his lines."

Fadumo, Alaina, and Kate looked at Alberto and then at each other. How were they going to include Alberto in their skit?

Instead of getting disappointed, they got to work. They gave Alberto some lines, taught him how to pronounce them, and helped him practice. He taught them a few Spanish words, and they worked those into the skit too. The group went through a practice presentation with the props, and everyone complimented each other on their hard work. And when Alaina noticed how well Alberto could draw, she asked him if he'd like to help draw the background setting. He agreed, and the results were great.

On the last day, they hung their beautiful backdrop, took turns recording, and finished up just in time. When it was their turn to share their skit with the class, all four of them were very proud of how it turned out.

Our goals don't always follow a straight path. Sometimes there are detours or unexpected twists and turns. It's okay to feel disappointed at first when things like this happen, but then it's time to problem-solve a way to make a Plan B. Many times, Plan B ends up working better than Plan A anyway.

JOT YOUR THOUGHTS

Write about a time you had to be flexible. For example, maybe you wrote an essay or story or poem, but it did not turn out how you had hoped. How did you handle that? Did you start over? Did you try to change the part you didn't like? Did you make it into something different?

When the Goal Is Not Your Own

It is one thing to work toward a goal that *you* want to accomplish. But what if you have to do something that you're not too excited about? It can be hard to be determined about a job that you don't really love to do. For example, maybe your teacher gives you a school assignment or your parent asks you to help with a household project. Maybe you are required to do a service project for a club or your faith community. If you're not excited about a task, but you have to do it, you might have to find different ways to stay determined. Read on for a few tips.

Focus on the Positive

As you work toward a goal, think about why you were asked to do it in the first place. Will it help someone who needs it? Will it help you learn a new skill or build up your knowledge about a subject? Even if the task is not one you would choose, chances are that there's a good reason it needs to be done, *and* that you can get something positive from the experience. Figure out what that is and focus on it.

Celebrate Success

Make sure you also celebrate as you go. Come up with a reward as you meet each goal or finish each step. You don't have to throw a party every time you learn a new thing, but maybe you could have an ice-cream treat, or paint your fingernails, or play your favorite video game after you do something well.

SOMETHING TO TRY

Create a celebration table or space at home or in your classroom, if your teacher agrees. You could decorate it with the words "Celebrate Success!" Get other students' help in filling it with all kinds of fun party blowers, instruments, stickers, or small treats. When you, or others, meet a goal or improve, you can go to the celebration table to celebrate your success.

Take Micro-Baby Steps

If the goal seems like it will take considerable time and effort, figure out ways to break it down. And if breaking your goal down into smaller steps doesn't motivate you enough, try taking a *micro*-baby step toward it. Think of a step that is *so* small you absolutely could not fail at it. (But only do this with something that isn't a pressing need!) You may take micro-baby steps for days and it won't seem daunting at all! You will probably be tempted to do more than one step a day. It may make you motivated to do multiple micro-steps at a time. When you look at a project in this way, it can take the "hugeness" out of the task.

For example, if you've ever had a parent tell you to clean the bedroom when it is extremely messy, it can seem like a huge, horrible headache. Ask if you can have a whole day to work on it. Then, each half hour, you could do one micro-baby step. Your first step might be to pick up one thing from the floor and put it away. Although cleaning may take longer with this process, it doesn't seem as hard.

CHAPTER 8

YOUR BEST IS YET TO COME!

Confronting your challenges and trying to improve and make progress can be hard, but with the skills you've learned in this book, you know how to approach those challenges and grow from them. You can feel more confident and less stressed.

Plus, the tools you are learning as you build your mindset power will help you your whole life! A growth mindset will help you in school, in your future jobs, and in your relationships with others. The coolest part is that you can take what you've learned and share it with those around you. You can spread positivity, encourage people when they have setbacks, and model growth-mindset thinking.

So if a growth mindset is so powerful, why doesn't *everyone* use it? Well, there are a lot of possible reasons:

- Some people are afraid to take risks.

- Some people are afraid to be wrong.

- Some people don't want to be embarrassed when their strategies don't work the first time.

- Some people get impatient when it takes too long to reach a goal.

- Some people don't want their goals badly enough.

- Some people don't know what tools to use.

- Some people don't feel comfortable asking for help.

- Some people don't know how to plan their first step.

- Some people just don't know how growth mindset can help them.

Here is the thing: **YOU are in charge of your mind and your mindset**. YOU get to choose if you go all-in on your goals. YOU get to decide if it is worth it to do the hard work necessary for growth.

When you are working to improve or learn something new, you have to leave your comfort zone. That means stepping outside of those areas where you feel safe and in control. It takes courage to challenge yourself to try things that may be scary at first. But with experience, you will find success. The more you do it, the easier it becomes to believe that your courage and hard work can lead to improvements, new adventures, new strengths, fun times, and confidence! When you believe in yourself and put in the work, good things will follow.

Things happen very fast in this world. We can cook a meal in a few minutes in a microwave oven. We have high-speed internet, so we can find answers to questions in a matter of seconds. You are growing up in a world where lots of people get what they want pretty quickly. They are used to "instant gratification."

Having a growth mindset doesn't mean you don't use any of the tools that make life more convenient. It just means that you also realize that some things, like learning a new skill or training your brain to do something differently, take time. They may take a *lot* of time.

If you decide you want to learn how to type 40 words per minute, you can't just sit at the computer and move your fingers really fast and hope for the best. No one will be able to read what you jumble together! You have to learn where the keys are, practice slowly and accurately, and eventually increase your speed. Your neurons will develop stronger connections, which will cause you to be able to type the correct words in less time, without having to think about it as much.

Putting in the time it takes to learn all the keys is an important step that you can't skip. Then you can set Effort Steps to gradually increase your speed. Your time invested up front will pay off because your practice will eventually allow you to type faster. That will save time on all your typed tasks in the future.

Many things worth learning do not have shortcuts. Instead of instant gratification, you have to *delay* gratification by putting in the time and effort and being patient. People who can do that are at an advantage. It's a skill that will help them in many ways throughout their lives.

Your Thoughts Are Powerful

Dr. Joe Dispenza is a guy who studies brains. Fascinating job, huh? He says the best way to predict your future is to create it yourself. He has done extensive brain research and says that everything starts with your thoughts. Maybe you start to think about something you'd like to accomplish. If you focus on those thoughts, they influence your choices. The choices you make affect what experiences you have. Your experiences help you form better habits, which reinforce what is going on in your brain.

For example, if you want to be a leader, you may think about that a lot. Maybe you think about leading a club or being the captain of a sports team. You think about it while you're at practice, in the middle of the night, and throughout the day. These thoughts cause you to want to make choices that move you closer to your goal. You'll start seeking experiences that grow the skills necessary for being a leader. You'll start noticing leadership skills in other people, when before you may not have paid as much attention. You might pick up a book to read about being a good leader or watch a video or two.

Before long, those thoughts of becoming the team captain come to your mind more readily. You replace some of your old habits with new habits—ones that may give you a better chance of being selected. You may start to serve your teammates more. Your coach may start to notice your leadership skills and praise you, which will reinforce your thoughts about wanting to become a leader. Your emotions and thoughts will grow stronger. The skills you are practicing will strengthen those neural pathways too.

It all started with your thoughts.

As you have learned, the pathways in your brain get stronger and stronger the more you use them. The thoughts and actions you take toward future goals all get processed together in your brain. This causes the neurons to fire and wire together. In this way, thinking about your future brings you closer to creating it for yourself.

If you think of who you want your best self to be, your body responds with feelings of joy, increased energy levels, and more focus. Your personality is actually formed by how you think, act, and feel. That's why it's important to figure out your hopes and ideas for the future.

Your new thoughts about growth mindset will lead to better choices. Your new choices will lead to better behavior. And your new behavior will lead to new and better habits in your life.

Are you ready to accept the challenge today to step out of your comfort zone and take on a growth mindset? You'll never regret working hard to grow your brain and learn new skills. You don't often hear anyone say, "I wish I didn't know how to solve hard math problems" or "I wish I wasn't so good at scoring three-point shots."

At the beginning of this book, you read that you will never reach your full potential. That means your best is truly yet to come. Think about Future You. What is that person good at? What is that person's attitude? As you think about that positive, brave person, make a plan to become that person.

1. Set goals that mean something to you. If you care enough about your goals, you will do what it takes to figure out the steps to get there.

2. Use a growth mindset as you work toward your goals.

3. Trust the Success Cycle (page 86): Try, fail, learn, improve, repeat. When you hit a bump in the road, be resilient.

4. When you achieve a goal, celebrate your success! Remember how wonderful it feels to crush a goal with hard work.

What you believe, you can achieve. Start with a goal you wrote in your notebook, and go for it!

I wish you well in your journey to use the power of your mindset to be the best you can be. Remember: In some small way, you can get better every day.

I know you will do great things!

RESOURCES

Books

How to Take the ACHE Out of Mistakes by Kimberly Feltes Taylor and Eric Braun
A humorous book to help you learn how to handle mistakes when they happen.

Mistakes That Worked by Charlotte Foltz Jones
Read about 40 familiar inventions that were invented by accident.

Your Fantastic, Elastic Brain by JoAnn Deak, Ph.D.
This book is all about your ability to grow and change your brain.

Nothing You Can't Do! by Mary Cay Ricci
Learn more about the power of adopting a growth mindset.

The Owner's Manual for Driving Your Adolescent Brain by JoAnn Deak, Ph.D., and Terrence Deak, Ph.D.
Take a deeper look at how your brain works.

Videos

"The Learning Brain"
youtu.be/cgLYkV689s4
Discover more about what the brain does and how you learn.

"Your Brain is Plastic"
youtu.be/5KLPxDtMqe8
Explore how your brain changes as you learn.

"The Mindset of a Champion"
youtu.be/px9CzSZsa0Y
Watch a fifth grader give a TEDxYouth talk about growth mindset.

"Growth Mindset vs. Fixed Mindset"
youtu.be/M1CHPnZfFmU
John Spencer explains the difference between a growth mindset and a fixed one.

INDEX

ABOUT THE AUTHOR

Shannon Anderson is a third-grade teacher who loves to encourage her students to develop a growth mindset and to learn from their growth spurts. She shares her Indiana home with her police-chief husband, two teen daughters, one very large dog, two cats, and two lizards. Shannon loves to write books for kids and read books that help her teach and learn in new ways.

Shannon earned her master's degree in education and holds a special license for teaching gifted and talented students. Some of her other books include *Y Is for Yet*, *Penelope Perfect*, and *Coasting Casey*, all Free Spirit titles. Shannon was honored to receive the 2018 JC Runyon Person of the Year award for her work helping kids with social and emotional needs. You can find out more about her at shannonisteaching.com.

Other Great Resources from Free Spirit

Get Organized Without Losing It
(Revised & Updated Edition)
by Janet S. Fox, illustrated by Steve Mark

For ages 8–13.
112 pp.; PB; full-color;
5⅛" x 7".

How to Take the ACHE Out of Mistakes
by Kimberly Feltes Taylor and Eric Braun, illustrated by Steve Mark

For ages 8–13.
128 pp.; PB; full-color;
5⅛" x 7".

See You Later, Procrastinator! (Get It Done)
by Pamela Espeland and Elizabeth Verdick, illustrated by Steve Mark

For ages 8–13.
112 pp.; PB; full-color;
5⅛" x 7".

Stress Can Really Get on Your Nerves!
(Revised & Updated Edition)
by Trevor Romain and Elizabeth Verdick, illustrated by Steve Mark

For ages 8–13.
184 pp.; PB; full-color;
5⅛" x 7".

Name and Tame Your Anxiety
A Kid's Guide
by Summer Batte, illustrated by Amberin Huq

For ages 9–13.
144 pp.; PB; 2-color; illust.;
6" x 9".

You're Smarter Than You Think
A Kid's Guide to Multiple Intelligences
(Revised & Updated Edition)
by Thomas Armstrong, Ph.D.

For ages 9–14.
208 pp.; PB; 2-color; illust.;
7" x 9".